The Population Census

Bernard Benjamin

HEINEMANN
LONDON

Heinemann Educational Books Ltd
LONDON MELBOURNE TORONTO
SINGAPORE JOHANNESBURG
EDINBURGH AUCKLAND
IBADAN NAIROBI
HONG KONG

SBN 435 82844 6

Published by Heinemann Educational Books Ltd
48 Charles Street, London W1X 8 AH
for the Social Science Research Council
State House, High Holborn, London W.C.1
Printed in Great Britain by
Cox & Wyman Ltd,
London, Fakenham and Reading

THE POPULATION CENSUS
an SSRC review of current research

SOCIAL SCIENCE RESEARCH COUNCIL

Reviews of Current Research

Contents

Foreword

Dr Benjamin's account of the practices and problems of the population census is one of a series of Social Science Research Council (SSRC) reviews dealing with various aspects of research in the social sciences. It differs from other publications in the series in that it is a description of the structure of an important source of information for many social scientists rather than a review of current research developments.

The subject was chosen by the Statistics Committee as one which although within the Committee's own field of reference was also of interest to social scientists working in other disciplines. Dr Benjamin was commissioned by the Statistics Committee to undertake the review in a personal capacity. Except where indicated, the views expressed are the personal opinions of the author and do not commit the SSRC or its Statistics Committee in any way. In particular, though the author's views are based on his experience as a Chief Statistician at the General Register Office from 1954 to 1963, they do not necessarily represent the official policy of that Office.

For the most part, the review is a factual statement of the technical and administrative aspects of the population census as normally conducted in Great Britain, with some reference to international comparability. The planning, conduct and analysis of the modern census requires sophisticated statistical thinking and a concentration on the specific uses to which the data are to be put. The author has endeavoured to spell this out in detail by reference to recent British experience.

JEREMY MITCHELL, *series editor*

The Population Census:

An account of procedures and utilization

1. *Introduction*

The population census which is taken in Great Britain and in most other developed countries of the world at regular intervals, usually of five or more years, is the primary source of information about the population of a country. Although the population census considered as a field operation has much in common with other kinds of field survey, it is nevertheless sharply distinguished by its traditional background, legal sanctions, coverage, and by the whole scale of the operation and the resources normally devoted to it, which permit a far greater content and depth of analysis than can normally be encompassed in other types of field study.

2. *Definition of a Census*

The words used internationally to describe a population census are as follows: a census of population may be defined as 'the total process of collecting, compiling, evaluating, analysing and publishing demographic, economic, and social data pertaining, at a specified time, to all persons in a country or in a well-delimited part of a country' (United Nations 1967).

Certain essential features follow from this definition. An official census is sponsored by the government of the area or of some larger region within which the area falls. The area covered is precisely defined. The principle of universality applies. The enumeration should either include every member of the community to which the census relates without omission or duplication or, if sampling is used, must give every member of a stratum equal likelihood of inclusion. The concept is one of individual rather than group enumeration. In this context the objection to group enumeration is that it tends to result in under-enumeration of the population (there are also statistical objections, e.g. the restriction of cross tabulation of individual characteristics). Relating the census to a point of time implies simultaneity of enumeration of all persons included in the census (or a close approximation to simultaneity). Population growth and change cannot be measured by a census taken at a single point of time; there is an implication also that there should be a series of censuses of regular periodicity.

3. *Legal Basis for the Census*

Population censuses carried out in Great Britain are at present covered by the Census Act of 1920, the main provisions of which are:

(i) power is given to the Registrars General of England and Wales, and Scotland, respectively, under the control and direction of the Minister of Health, to hold enumerations at intervals of not less than five years;

(ii) the direction to take a census is to be by Order in Council, and may be for great Britain or any part of Great Britain (the minimum time interval is specific to a particular part; i.e. a census cannot be 'taken in any part of Great Britain in any year unless at the commencement of that year at least five years have elapsed since the commencement of the year in which a census was last taken in that part . . .');

(iii) the questions to be asked at any census are to be prescribed by the Order in Council, but must fall within the following general scope of topics as listed in the Schedule to the 1920 Act:

(a) Names, sex, age.

(b) Occupation, profession, trade or employment.

(c) Nationality, birthplace, race, language.

(d) Place of abode, character of dwelling.

(e) Condition as to marriage, relation to head of family, issue born in marriage.

(f) Any other matter with respect to which it is desirable to obtain statistical information with a view to ascertaining the social or civil condition of the population. (Any questions specified under this heading come under the close scrutiny of Parliament, since these must be the subject of an affirmative resolution of both Houses.)

(iv) The Registrar General may at the cost of any local authority or private person satisfy a 'reasonable' request for statistical information derived from the census but not contained in the published reports. (The use of this provision has increased and is likely to increase as a result of an increased demand for data specific to a local or sectional population but not of sufficient general interest to warrant incorporation in the main tabulations of the census.)

4. *The Scope of Census Inquiries*

The scope of paragraph (f) of the Schedule to the 1920 Act is very wide, but it has to be borne in mind that two important restrictions may operate to limit the amount of information which can be sought. First, the requirement that these topics shall be the subject of affirmative resolution by both Houses of Parliament means that any topic which may offend public opinion or which appears to be too remotely connected with the main objective of the census as an instrument of social administration is likely to be ruled out. Secondly, census questions which supply information essential to the business of government or directly useful to the community at large (which pays taxes to meet the bill), are likely to come before other topics, especially those related to a specialized demand and not commanding wide interest. Further, a ceiling is bound to be placed upon the total cost of the census, and since processing cost is roughly proportional to the number of questions, this number is bound to be effectively limited.

Apart from these considerations, there is a practical restriction on the extent of the census inquiries. Merely to ask an additional question in the census schedule does not ensure a correct answer. Any progressive elaboration of the schedule is likely to reach a stage at which indifference, if not resentment, will introduce inaccuracy, and this may cause doubt to be cast on the validity of the whole enumeration. This is a very important consideration where the householder is required to complete the schedule, but even where canvassers are employed, steps have to be taken to reduce the burden of questions to be directed to any one household. If the number of aspects on which population statistics are sought (additional to the basic details of age, sex, marital condition, size of household and dwelling, etc.) are too numerous to be covered at one census without excessive complexity in the schedule, it is better to cover them some at a time by a set of supplemental questions at successive censuses, especially if these by virtue of their simplicity can be held more frequently than otherwise.

Apart from the restraints imposed by national needs and national resources, and by the willingness of the population to respond there is the further consideration of international comparability (and of international recommendations to that end).

5. *Consultation*

In Great Britain all these matters have ultimately to be weighed by the Minister of Health who is responsible for proposing a list of census topics to Parliament, on the recommendation of the Government Department (at present the General Register Office) in whose charge lies the conduct of the population census. These recommendations are constructed on as wide a basis of consultation as is practicable.

Before discussing this process of consultation, two important points must be made. First, it has always been considered inadvisable and uneconomical to attempt to separate people from the dwellings in which they are found; the housing census is *not* conducted separately from the population census as it is in some countries. The separation is considered statistically inadvisable because the household is a population group and the generation of households is determined only partly by changes in population structure and only partly by changes in housing stock; the two sources of change are most appropriately regarded as part of one whole system. The separation is uneconomic because many of the characteristics of housing require to be cross-classified with population characteristics (e.g. dwelling size (rooms) against household size (persons), tenure (owned or rented) against occupation group of chief economic supporter). A housing census if conducted separately would have its cost (in money terms and in strain upon public goodwill) increased beyond that of the strictly housing content by the necessity to repeat many of the questions asked in the population census.

The second point is that there is a back-log of experience if not on topic *need*, at least on topic *feasibility*. It is the regular (and very desirable) practice of the General Register Office to hold an inquest on the whole census operation as soon as the data processing stage has been reached. Evidence is taken from a representative cross-section of the field staff while the difficulties of interpretation and response are still fresh in the memory. Reports are also available of the defects in schedules encountered in validation and coding prior to the transference of data to punched cards. All this information and the assessment of it is well documented for subsequent reference. In respect of any topic, therefore, on which questions have been asked in the past, there is considerable information of the difficulties of response, the circumstances in which these difficulties were experienced and the efficacy of any steps taken to surmount them.

Apart from the records of the census evaluation the General Register Office will also know from its own data processing commitments and its provision of basic data for further exploitation by other Government Departments or local authorities or outside bodies, just what use has been made of information gathered on a particular topic. Some assessment can therefore be made of the value of the information and whether it was worth the cost of collection.

Starting from this point the General Register Office begins the process of consultation some four years or so before the date of the census; indeed, as soon as is practicable after the previous census. A general approach is made to Government Departments, local authority organizations (and some large individual authorities), university departments, research centres, trade and professional organizations and learned societies, etc., to seek their views on the scope (in topics) of the census. It is essential, in this process, to seek not only suggestions about new topics or the repetition of previous topics but also (given a ceiling on total coverage) to enable these suggestions to be marked in priority. The questions to be answered in respect of any suggestion are:

(1) Precisely what information is required?

It is helpful to present this in an outline tabulation form

since this not only assists the appreciation of usefulness but may later be vital to the proper design of the census question.

(2) Who wants the information?

Other things being equal, a specialized demand will have lower priority than a general demand. Often other things are *not* equal. A specialized demand though coming from a narrow section of the community may be weighted on other counts, e.g. the ultimate value to the community and the inability to obtain the information in any other way.

(3) What is the purpose of the information and how will it be used to achieve this purpose?

This helps to give definition to the answer to question 1 above.

(4) Is the information required on a national scale or only for a part of the country?

Questions of national relevance must have higher priority than those relevant to a more restricted area for which an ad hoc survey might be more applicable.

(5) Is the information on the particular topic essentially to be related to other census information?

If the proposed question stands on its own without the need to relate it to other questions then the use of the population census as the vehicle is contra-indicated. It could be handled by ad hoc survey.

It is desirable in order to make the best use of the census that the census schedule should represent a battery of questions the answers to which require to be related, in part, if not in total.

To this information the General Register Office will add its own initial assessment of the relative cost of the proposed topics in terms of the additional burden which may be placed on enumerators and the additional data-processing and publication. This assessment may be later modified, for example as a feed-back from the pilot field trials, before the census schedule is finally designed.

A judgement then has to be made as to the topics which will be recommended for parliamentary approval after having regard to all this information and the general considerations already discussed in Section 4. Before making this judgement it is necessary to test the weight of evidence by further consultation. In the British context there are a number of possible avenues to follow. A statement of possible proposals can be sent to all those from whom views were originally solicited as a representative sample of informed census data users, seeking their general reactions. An inspired but unofficial article can be placed in a social, economic or demographic journal to see what reaction it provokes. More constructively an advisory panel of important users and survey experts can be constituted to work its way through the proposals at a series of meetings. This panel would be free to suggest amendments or entirely new proposals. At the same time, for obvious reasons, the Head of Government Statistical Services will consider the relevance of the census proposals to Government needs within a suitable interdepartmental committee. All these consultations will embrace other aspects of data collection; for example grid referencing and the possible use of sampling (to which further reference will be made later in this manual).

When the census proposals have been finally agreed at officer level they must be agreed with the Minister of Health[1] and through him with the Cabinet prior to the introduction of the necessary draft Order in Council in the two Houses of Parliament. At this stage of course the cost and the method of

---

[1] Currently there is one Department of Health *and* Social Security, though of the several Ministers attached thereto under the Secretary of State for Social Services one is specifically responsible for Health.

enumeration have to be politically acceptable as well as the census questions.

6. *Sampling*

Before discussing census topics in detail it is convenient to dispose of a number of general considerations about sampling in enumeration.

The largest work load of the population census is in the enumeration in the field. Conversion of the documentation to computer input, i.e. coding and card punching, is also a heavy load but while the reduction of numbers enumerated eases this load, the converse does not apply – a reduction of work at the data-processing stage has no effect on the major burden of field work. There are, moreover, developing possibilities for the reduction of the work of data-processing; for example, electronic document-reading to obviate manual card punching and automatic coding to reduce manual coding to at least the less common categories. Both of these possibilities would tip the scale in favour of canvass (inter-views to complete schedules) rather than self-enumeration (completion of schedules by householders), as at present practised in Great Britain; indeed they would probably render self-enumeration impracticable. They would certainly increase the burden in the field. It is therefore necessary to concentrate on the field.

The case for sampling in enumeration is that every schedule that can be saved in the field is a reduction of burden on both the public and officials. Sampling saves work and money. It fosters good relations with the public because it demonstrates official economy. It raises official morale because it demon-strates a contemporary professional and intensively practical approach to the conduct of the census. This demonstration can only succeed, indeed sampling itself can only succeed, if the field work is under adequate professional direction.

9

There is the additional argument that the largest area of risk of error is in the field. Office training, good direction with hierarchical reference of difficult cases (i.e. the reference of more difficult cases to higher levels of expertise) and well thought out conventions together with the application of quality control techniques can reduce coding and other manual data processing errors on individual items of a record to an acceptable level. Computer editing can deal with recognizable inconsistencies between items of a record. Nothing can be done however to replace a completely omitted record or to rectify a plausible yet falsely completed record. Fewer but better identified households and fewer but more carefully supervised interrogations are likely to mean higher quality of response and clearer data.

There are arguments against sampling in the field.

One argument is likely to be that while the census is an excellent *frame* for sampling there is, in the absence of a continuous population record (of the type operated in the highly centralized conditions of Scandinavia and the Netherlands), no obvious sampling frame for the census itself, i.e. there is no up-to-date list of *all* households to draw a sample from. Only the census itself establishes such a list.

This argument was accepted in 1961 when a few census questions were addressed to all households but the majority of the questions (including the more difficult ones) were addressed only to 10 per cent of households. The 10 per cent sample was effectively established *in the process of identifying all* households. This was achieved very simply by the following process:

(i) Each enumerator was given a pack of schedules more than sufficient in number for all households in his district.

(ii) The pack consisted of a mixture of sample and non-sample schedules arranged in such a way that starting from the top of the pack the xth, $x + 10^{th}$, $x + 20^{th}$ – was a sample schedule, x being a random number less than 10.[1]

(iii) The enumerator was instructed to proceed round his district taking successive households in an *orderly* way and to hand out schedules consistently from the top of the pack, i.e. issuing them in the prescribed order.

(iv) The enumerator was required to list all dwellings and the constituent households to whom he had, following the instruction of (iii) above, issued sample schedules.

If the enumerator followed these rules and if he followed his normal procedure of working systematically round his district (identifying buildings, dwellings within buildings, households within dwellings) he should have selected a representative unbiased sample. But it is possible that he did *not* always follow the rules.

The following statement appears in the introductions to the table volumes of the 1961 Census:

BIAS

After the 1961 Census, the 10 per cent sample was checked for bias by comparing certain items of information common to the full census and the sample census. One such comparison showed clearly that the sample of households was biased. Although the total number of households in the sample is almost exactly one-tenth of the total in the whole country, the distribution of households by number of persons and number of rooms occupied is distorted. The amount of bias is shown in the table below. There is considerable under-representation of one-person households and of large households. For any

---

[1] H.M. Stationery Office prepared packs with sample schedules in the 10th, 20th, etc., positions. The census officer was given a list of enumeration districts with a random number x attached to each. He had only to remove from one pack (10 − x) schedules and add the requisite number of whole packs, before supplying the individual enumerator.

Percentage Excess in 10 per cent sample when compared with one-tenth of the full count figures.

Persons in the household	Number of rooms occupied							All households
	1	2	3-4	5	6	7-8	9 and over	
1	—11	—11	—8	—7	—4	—2	+10	—8
2-6	—7	—3	+0	+1	+5	+9	+20	+2
7 and over	—22	—28	—14	—10	—9	—7	—1	—10
All households	—10	—6	—1	+0	+3	+8	+17	+0

stated size of household there is a clear gradient from too few households occupying few rooms towards too many households with large numbers of rooms.

To allow for this bias, correcting factors have been calculated which users can apply to the 10 per cent census data. It was not a practical proposition to calculate such factors for every entry in the tables. Instead they have been obtained for certain of the more important marginal totals.

In the General Report on the 1961 Census further details have been given. There was systematic under-representation of old people, of the widowed and divorced population of all ages and of single males aged 25 and over. There were small deficiencies of young married people and children under 5 years of age. In compensation, the sample contained too many married people between 30 and 70 and too many young people between the ages of 5 and 20. (All these differences are the expected concomitants of the under-representation of one-person households and of large households.) There was a deficiency in the sample of people in hotels and boarding-houses; as some of these households were originally enumerated as private households (before the households were reclassified under the processing convention that a household with five or more boarders should be treated as a boarding-house) part of this deficiency too is attributable to the general under-representation of large households. There was a deficiency in the sample of persons born outside England and Wales, especially Nigeria, Cyprus, Pakistan and the Caribbean area. The bias tended to be greater in rural districts.

One immediate observation may be made. The allegation of bias rests on a comparison between the 90 per cent and 10 per cent schedules and these two types of schedule were completed under very different conditions. The 10 per cent sample schedule provided for the recording of those members of the de jure household who were temporarily absent on census night; the non-sample schedule did not. The de facto household was much more sharply defined in the sample schedule because every member of the de jure household could be accounted for either as present (de facto) or absent (entered in part III of the schedule). The comparison is therefore *not* between like and like.

The General Register Office admit that it is 'possible that there was a tendency for households with a member away on census night to record themselves as N person households on the E.10 form in the sample with one person added in the absent member section but (wrongly) as a household with $(N + 1)$ persons present on an E.90 form'. They add that 'this phenomenon could help to account for the relative shortage of one-person households in the sample but does not contribute towards the similar shortage of households with large numbers of persons'. This is true. It is possible to consider another aspect of the non-comparability of response to the two types of census schedule, namely, that if there is any tendency, from carelessness or evasion, to omit some persons from large households, this is likely to affect the E.10 more than the E.90 because the E.10 made a greater demand on the householder's knowledge of other members of the household. Apart from these factors, there may have been bias introduced by departure from the rules for the distribution of sample schedules (as has already been indicated). These departures include:

(1) Faulty sorting of the pack of schedules, i.e. sample schedules in wrong frequency or periodicity.

(2) 'Drop outs', i.e. a schedule is left but not collected because the householder moves on. This is more likely to have occurred if the householder was a temporary occupant either singly as a lodger or in the group of boarders in multiple occupation of a dwelling.

(3) 'Drop ins', i.e. completion of a schedule which the enumerator for the district did not deliver but which the household moving in had brought with it from a distribution elsewhere.

(4) The enumerator may have exhausted his pack and then have completed the distribution from an unsorted collection of spare schedules.

(5) 'Switching', i.e. the enumerator may have interfered with the strict ordering of the pack (*a*) in order to avoid giving the more complex sample schedule to a larger household (especially an immigrant household) or to an elderly person living alone, if he thought this would cause difficulty or hostility; (*b*) in order to omit households of unusual structure from the sample so that in his view the sample would be more 'representative' (equating 'usual' and 'representative' is a common failing in the lay mind). It is thought that 'switching' would occur more frequently where the enumerator had prior knowledge of the character of the household on which he was calling and that since this condition would be more likely to be satisfied in rural districts this would explain, in part, the greater amount of bias in those districts. It was also thought that in urban areas there would be more uniformity in

households and therefore less opportunity to justify switching.

In the event the General Register Office have admitted that, to the extent that it can be measured, the amount of this bias was not great, and that it probably caused more damage to the census through the delay involved in assessing its extent than by the actual effect on census statistics. Even this delay was less than that associated with other causes, e.g. computer programming. It would appear that only rarely if at all are these correction factors sufficiently different from unity to lead to difficulty in applying the census results to practical problems of administration and policy.

In the light of the available evidence the 1961 experience is not a case against sampling; it is a case against the use of a simple sampling procedure without the safeguard of a pilot to test its reliability and to provide the evidence of likely 'bending' of the rules needed for effective education of enumerators against this risk.

The 1966 experience was different. The census was entirely on a sample basis. The sample was selected from a two-part frame (1) the major part – the 1961 census list of dwellings; (2) a small part – the post-1961 dwellings listed in rating valuation records. The details are given in the explanatory notes to census publications and it is unnecessary to go into refinements.

In the event the sample was estimated to be short by $1\frac{1}{4}$ per cent in private dwellings and $1\frac{2}{3}$ per cent in population. To keep this shortfall in perspective it has to be borne in mind that as recently as 1960 a *full* census of the U.S.A. carried out in part by mailing contact and in part by canvass was estimated to have under-enumerated the population by 1·7 to 2·0 per cent. This was an improvement on the *full* census of 1950 when at least 3 per cent and possibly 5 per cent of households were missed. So that to treat the 1966 shortfall in

England and Wales as a very serious error, as some have done, is hardly justifiable and would not be a mature view.

An analysis of the 1966 census shortfall indicates that two-thirds may be attributed to deficiencies in the sample frame and one-third to errors during the 1966 enumeration.

The errors in the 1966 sample frame can be analysed in the following way:

(*a*) Deficiency in the 1961 census as a sample frame due to exclusion of:
   (i) Dwellings missed in the 1961 enumeration.
   (ii) Some dwellings enumerated as vacant in 1961 but occupied in 1966 which were not put into the frame owing to weakness in 1961 clerical procedures.
   (iii) Some dwellings which were *non*-residential in 1961 but which had become residential between 1961 and 1966.
   (iv) Some dwellings under repair or reconstruction in 1961 and since made habitable.

(*b*) Exclusion of new property which had not got on to the Valuation List in March 1966 when this List was examined.

(*c*) Omission of isolated caravans, vagrants, etc.

Most of these errors could have been avoided by better organization and none represents a valid argument against sampling. Not much could be done about dwellings which were missed in the 1961 enumeration and are therefore entirely outside the sampling frame but better work on the ground could have remedied the other sources of deficiency. In the light of knowledge of the sources of deficiency (which are nothing to do with sampling itself) one can be surprised that the deficiency was so small.

Certain technical problems arise if sampling is used. If, as is more convenient, systematic rather than random sampling is adopted, steps have to be taken to avoid the bias which is often associated with the former method. In the United States census of 1950, for example, the conditions under which new enumeration sheets were completed gave rise to some degree of association between population characteristics and the order of line on the sheet. This did not seriously affect the 20 per cent sample, but it was found that for the $3\frac{1}{3}$ per cent sample, which consisted of the persons listed on the last sample line of each schedule, persons in small households were under-represented (by about 4 per cent) as a result of the instruction given to enumerators to start a new sheet whenever the set of twelve housing lines on the back of the schedule had been completed, thus leaving some lines blank on the front of the schedules where population questions were recorded. In the self-enumeration type of census (as in the United Kingdom) with a household schedule there is a choice between (i) a systematic selection of serially listed households using complementary numbers to avoid bias (as in the selection of the 1951 1 per cent sample); (ii) some system of shuffling schedules of different types before distribution as in 1961; (iii) the central selection of addresses of dwellings and the issue of those addresses to enumerators, as in 1966. The scale of the operation militates against refined methods and some degree of departure from high standards of randomization has to be accepted.

Method (iii) raises again the question of a sampling frame. In market research where distributions are important and not absolute numbers, considerable use is made of electoral registers and there is no doubt that this use has contributed much to the better up-dating of those registers. The more a record is known to be used by the public, the more interest is taken by officials to see that it is as free as possible from public criticism. The census however has to provide the benchmarks for year-to-year population estimates of local authorities and these estimates provide the basis for central government financial grants. The local authorities have therefore to be convinced that failing a total head count, any method of sampling can lead to a grossed-up population estimate of high precision; they would certainly wish to be convinced that there is no bias in a downward direction such as might occur if a deficient electoral register were used as the sampling frame. It is very likely that in a highly mobile population electoral registers will always be deficient. This underlines the advantage possessed by those countries (for example, the Netherlands, Denmark, Sweden, Norway) which are able to maintain systems of continuous population registers, with sanctions to ensure completeness, in that they have a standing and up-to-date sampling frame for the population census and other national and local surveys.

In the absence of a standing list of households Method (i) requires in addition to the main enumeration a prior contact with households such as normally takes place when schedules are delivered. In Great Britain it would not be an improvement on Method (ii). The latter has the merit of simplicity but, as has already been indicated, it can only ensure complete coverage if (*a*) the identification of dwellings and the households in them is accurate and complete (a prerequisite for census accuracy whether or not sampling is used) and (*b*) if the enumerators, on the basis of training and understanding, are sufficiently disciplined to stick to the rules for census schedule distribution. In the U.S.A. in 1960 use was made of the postal authority to make an initial contact with households (i.e. all households to which mail is, as of census data, normally delivered. An initial letter and simple self-enumeration form (prepaid reply) was sent to all households through the ordinary mail services in this way. On the basis of the replies as a total frame a sample was then selected for interview visit to collect the remaining information. The method appears to have been successful. The recruitment of enumerators to make this preliminary encounter (as in Method (iii) above) would have been costly because households in the U.S.A. are on the average farther apart than in Great Britain, and less efficient because they would not start with the advantage possessed by the mail men, i.e. prior knowledge of households to whom they normally delivered mail.

The U.S.A. has an immense advantage over Great Britain in that it has a permanent census bureau with a field survey force of its own (albeit mainly for employment survey purposes) whereas in Great Britain this highly technical operation of the census is imposed on a Department which is regarded by the Treasury as predominantly administrative, and imposed, moreover, on each occasion as if it were an isolated event. The time-table suffers from the traumatic redeployment of staff that has to take place and though there are statisticians there is no permanent or sufficient supply of skills in sampling and interviewing techniques or in carto-graphy.[1] The General Register Office is therefore ill-equipped for the careful planning that is a prerequisite of successful sampling.

If sampling is used steps must be taken to reduce sampling errors, e.g. by regression methods based on relationship of sample values to values recorded in complete enumeration and by intelligent choice of sampling fraction.

It is important too that the published tables should in-dicate clearly that they are based on sample data and the tables should be accompanied by adequate explanation of the method of grossing up (if the figures *are* grossed up). There should also be adequate notes on the method of

---

[1] The General Register Office point out that since 1968 they have had two graduate research officers qualified in geography and sociology to study census methodology and there is now also regular consultation with the Social Survey. This development is acknow-ledged and welcomed but the general comment in relation to past censuses and especially to the 1966 sample census still applies.

calculating the sampling errors remaining present in the published figures (see Appendix A).

A further problem is presented by the need for cross-tabulation of several factors; this can only be effected for those members of the population who have been asked all of the relevant questions. This need does, therefore, operate as a serious restraint upon the possible sharing out of questions to ease the burden of response; for most of the answers asked for in British censuses, such as those on occupation, industry, education, require correlation one with another in tabulation and the questions must all appear on the same schedule. In practice therefore sampling would be used not to increase the total questions asked but to reduce the total number of persons required to answer any questions at all other than those which are involved in the simplest exact count of heads. It may well be that despite a convincing case for conducting the census entirely on a sample basis such a count will be required as a sure starting-point for the inter-censal estimates of local populations that form the basis of Exchequer Grants in Great Britain. It would be necessary in that event to have two schedules, one containing only questions on age, sex, marital condition, and addressed to $(100 - x)$ per cent of the population, and another containing the full battery of questions but addressed to only x per cent of the population (where x is determined by reference to the likely sampling errors in the smallest cells of the tabulation)

7. *Historical development of subject scope of censuses in Great Britain*

In England and Wales and Scotland the first census was in 1801 and was repeated thereafter at decennial intervals until 1961 with a break in 1941 because the country was then totally mobilized for World War II so that even if manpower could have been spared the results would not have represented a normal picture. The census of 1801 counted the number of males and females of each house and family and the number of persons engaged in agriculture, trade, manufacture or handicraft and other occupations not specially classified. In 1821 information was first sought as to ages, but it was left optional whether this should be furnished or not. Before the 1841 Census the civil registration of births, deaths and marriages had been instituted in England and Wales and the newly appointed local Registrars replaced the parish overseers as the officers responsible for conducting the census. In addition the duty of completing the enumeration form for each family was delegated to the head of the household instead of to an official, thus enabling simultaneous entry to be made of every person. In Scotland civil registration was not established until 1855 and the census of 1841 was entrusted to the official schoolmaster or other fit person. The census of 1851 was carried out under William Farr's supervision and was more detailed than earlier enumerations. Information was obtained of occupation, birthplace, relationship (husband, wife, etc.), marital condition (married, widowed, bachelor, etc.), education and the number of persons deaf and dumb or blind. At this census under the powers given by the Census Act, the precise age at last birthday of each person in the country was first demanded. The Scottish Census of 1861 was the first to be conducted by the Registrar-General for Scotland.

In the census report of 1881, the age and sex distribution of the population of each urban and rural sanitary authority as constituted that year was given for the first time.

At the census of 1891 the schedule contained new questions as to number of rooms and of their occupants in all tenements with less than five rooms, and as to the important occupational distinction between employers, employees and those working on their own account.

In 1901 no further additions were made to the subjects of

inquiry, but provision was made in a single enactment for taking the Census throughout Great Britain. In 1911 a number of important changes were made. The difficulty of defining a 'house' was avoided by the enumeration for each urban and rural district of the number of various classes of buildings used as dwellings – ordinary dwelling houses, blocks of flats and the separate flats or dwellings composing them, shops, institutions, etc., with the corresponding populations. The limited accommodation inquiry of the 1891 Census was extended to tenements of all sizes. The industry as well as the occupation of each worker was recorded. The tabulations gave ages in single years of life instead of groupings. The most important development was a detailed inquiry into fertility. The following questions were asked in respect of every married woman:

(1) Duration of marriage in completed years.
(2) The number of children born alive to the present marriage who:
    (*a*) were still alive at the census;
    (*b*) had died before the census.

This information when related to other census data as to age, marital status, occupation, etc., enabled a study of area and social class differences in marriage and child bearing experience to be attempted.

Up to 1911 each census had been covered by a separate Act of Parliament, but the Census Act of 1920 gave power to hold periodical enumerations at intervals of not less than five years and covered not only the 1921 Census but future censuses. The Act states that the questions to be asked at any census are to be prescribed by Order in Council, as already set out in Section 3 of this manual.

In designing the schedule for the census of 1921 it was thought that a point had been reached in progressive enlargement of census inquiries at which any further addition to the total quantity of information might lead to indifference or resistance and consequent inaccuracy. Most of the changes were therefore in the nature of substitutions. The fertility inquiry of 1911 was not repeated on the grounds that in 1921 such an inquiry would have reflected not normal experience but the disturbance of World War I, but instead the schedule was designed to seek dependency information, i.e. details of all living children and step-children under the age of 16 for each married man, widower or widow on the schedule (whether these children were enumerated on the same schedule or not). Such information of the numbers and ages of existing children according to age and marital status of parent was essential to the development of national widows' and orphans' pensions then contemplated. The questions as to infirmities (blind, deaf, dumb and lunatics) of earlier censuses were dropped since it was generally recognized that there was a natural reluctance to disclose that members of the family were afflicted in these ways and that data could not be expected to be reliable; but a new question was added as to place of work. A new industrial and occupational classification was employed.

1931 CENSUS

Although as at previous censuses the 1931 enumeration was on a de facto basis, i.e. each person was enumerated where found at the time of the census instead of at the usual place of residence (referred to as the de jure basis) for the first time a question was inserted in the schedule asking for a statement of the address of usual residence of each person enumerated in the household.

The 1931 schedule omitted any inquiry into education, workplace and either dependency or fertility, and was thus simpler than in 1921. This reduction in scope was made partly for economy and also because it was anticipated that in future more frequent enumerations would be made and that emphasis would be placed at different times on different additions to this minima in order to spread the complete survey over several censuses. (It was intended to hold a census in 1936 but it was later decided not to fulfil this intention.) As a reflection of the economic depression of the time the 1931 schedule was extended to include particular mention of those 'out of work'.

NATIONAL REGISTRATION 1939

As part of general security measures during World War II every civilian person in Great Britain on 29 September 1939 had to be recorded on a National Register. The head of each household was required to complete a schedule similar to that of a normal census, showing the name, age, sex, date of birth, marital condition, occupation and national service commitment of every member of the household. For individual identification each person received a card bearing a registered number, name and address and date of birth. In 1944 the National Register Volume was published showing the civilian population of each area, in sex and age-groups; no information was given as to occupation.

THE 1951 CENSUS

The enumeration was carried out as at midnight 8/9 April 1951 in England, Wales and Scotland. In addition to the customary questions as to age, sex, marital condition, occupation, etc., certain special questions were included. These were:

FERTILITY: Married women under the age of 50 were asked to state:

 (i) the date of present marriage (and if married more than once the date of the first marriage),
 (ii) the total children born alive to her (all marriages),

(iii) whether she had given birth to a live-born child during the last twelve months.

EDUCATION: All persons were asked whether they were attending an educational establishment for the purpose of instruction at the date of the census and if so whether full-time or part-time. Persons not then receiving full-time instruction were asked to state the age at which such full-time instruction ceased.

HOUSEHOLD ARRANGEMENTS: Heads of households were asked to indicate the availability to the household of the following facilities:

(i) a piped water supply within the dwelling (as distinct from a tap in the yard or public standpipe),
(ii) cooking stove with an oven,
(iii) kitchen sink with drainpipe leading outside (not a wash-basin),
(iv) water-closet (not an earth or chemical closet),
(v) a fixed bath with waste pipe leading outside.

The question on place of work, last asked at the 1921 Census, was reintroduced.

As in earlier census enumerations the schedule was completed by the head of household and was collected by a paid enumerator who gave such assistance as was necessary on matters of interpretation regarding the completion of the form.

An important innovation was the preparation of advance tabulations of the census results almost within a year of the census date by selecting and processing a 1 per cent sample of the schedules. Two volumes of tables were produced during 1952. The first (Census 1951, Great Britain, 1 per cent Sample Tables, Part I) gave a detailed description of the method adopted to ensure that the sample was representative, of the design of the tabulations and of the factors to be borne in mind in their interpretation; it included tabulations of ages, marital condition, occupations, industries, housing and household arrangements. The second volume covered household composition, birthplace, education and fertility. Naturally the amount of detail given and the degree of area breakdown was limited by the fact that the data were limited in number to 1 per cent of the total and the tabulations were preliminary and did not replace the full tabulations which were to come.

THE 1961 CENSUS

The enumeration of 1961 was notable for the following innovations:

(1) Three important additions to the range of questions asked at previous censuses. These were:

> (i) Tenure of dwelling (whether (*a*) owner-occupied, or (*b*) rented and if so, whether from a private landlord, or local authority, or with a farm, shop, or business premises, or (*c*) by virtue of employment). This was to provide a measure of the sizes of these groups so that the government would know the strengths of the various interests it had to protect.

> (ii) Change of usual address in the previous year. This was to fill a long-felt gap in knowledge about internal migration in the country; the main streams of movement and the characteristics of the movers (types of household, ages, occupations).

> (iii) Scientific and technological qualifications. This was to provide more comprehensive statistics on scientific manpower than was previously available.

(2) The use of sampling in the enumeration for the first time. In 1951 a 1 per cent sample of the completed tabulations had been used to produce advance tabulations but every household had been required to complete the full

schedule. In 1961 it was decided to reduce the burden on the public by imposing a full schedule on only 10 per cent of households, selected systematically and to require the remainder to answer only a limited range of personal questions (sex, age, marital condition, birthplace, citizenship, and, for married women, number of live-born children).

(3) Provision in the 10 per cent sample schedule for statement of members of the household absent on census day, so that for the first time the de jure household could be compared with the de facto household to which previous censuses had been restricted.

(4) The conduct of a post-enumeration survey to detect errors of response. This was on a sample basis and in two parts (*a*) a careful re-trawl of the selected areas as a check that every household was enumerated, (*b*) interviews with a small subsample of households to check any errors of response to individual questions.

THE 1966 CENSUS

The 1966 Census (midnight 24/25 April 1966) was the first to take place after an interval as short as five years from the previous census and the first to be conducted entirely on a 10 per cent sample basis. The following questions, not asked at previous censuses, were asked:

Of the head of each household in the sample
Cars, garaging

(*a*) How many cars, including vans, taxed wholly or in part as private vehicles, are owned or used exclusively by you and members of your household?

(*b*) For each car or van entered at (*a*) show where it is normally kept overnight by writing 'yes' at (i), (ii), (iii) or (iv), or by giving details at (v). If there are more than two vehicles give answers for only two of them.

	1st vehicle	2nd vehicle
(i) In a garage or carport within the grounds of your dwelling	———————	———————
(ii) In a garage or carport elsewhere	———————	———————
(iii) Within the grounds of your dwelling but not in a garage or carport	———————	———————
(iv) On the road, street or verge	———————	———————
(v) Elsewhere – please give details	———————	———————

Of each person aged 15 and over
Travel to work

What method of transport does the person normally use for the largest part, by distance, of the journey to the place of work given in reply to question 15 (i.e. the place of primary employment) ———————

Employment additional to the main occupation

(*a*) Did the person do any other work for payment or profit during the week ended 23 April 1966 in addition to the work detailed in reply to questions 12 and 13 (the main occupation) Write 'yes' or 'no' ———————

(*b*) If 'yes' was any of the additional work as an employee? Write 'yes' or 'no' ———————

The question first introduced in 1961 as to ownership and renting of accommodation was retained. Certain questions were sharpened in definition as a result of experience in 1961; these included the questions on household amenities and the questions on employment. The underlying circumstances will be discussed later in a further treatment of census concepts and definitions (Section 9).

8. *International Recommendations*

The Statistical Office of the United Nations have published a report on 'Principles and Recommendations for the 1970 Population Censuses' in which they submit a list of 'recommended' and 'other useful topics' (the former being distinguished by asterisks). The Report states that these are the topics 'which have emerged after decades of census experience as of the greatest utility for both national and international purposes'.

Topics which appear on the questionnaire	*Derived Topics*
Geographic characteristics	
* Place where found at time of census	* Total population
* Place of usual residence	* Locality subdivision
* Place of birth	* Urban and rural subdivision
Duration of residence	
Place of previous residence	
Place of work	
Personal and household characteristics	
* Sex	* Household composition
* Age	Family composition
* Relationship to head of household	
Relationship to head of family	
* Marital status	
Age at marriage	
Duration of marriage	
Marriage order	
* Children born alive	
* Children living	
Citizenship	
* Literacy	
* School attendance	

* Educational attainment
  Educational qualifications
  National and/or ethnic group
  Language
  Religion

Economic characteristics

* Type of activity   Socio-economic status
* Occupation   Dependency
* Industry
* Status (as employer, employee, etc.)
  Main source of livelihood

For particular application to Europe these recommendations have been reviewed by a Working Group on Population Censuses set up by the Conference of European Statisticians (a representative body of official statisticians which meets under the auspices of the U.N. Economic Commission for Europe). Their list distinguishes between *basic topics* which are of general interest and value to European countries and additional topics which though useful are of less importance. The grouping of topics is also changed.

In the European geographical group 'Duration of residence' becomes an 'additional' topic as also does 'place of birth' as distinct from 'country of birth' which *is* basic. Under 'personal characteristics', 'citizenship' is shown as basic. 'Religion' and 'mental or physical disabilities' appear as 'additional' topics. In the European list the 'main source of livelihood' and 'dependency relationship' appear as 'basic' and under the heading of additional topics reference is made to 'length of unemployment (or unemployment as such)', 'time worked', 'income', 'identity of actual main supporter of dependent person', 'secondary occupation', 'secondary industry', 'size of enterprise', 'secondary status'. Under the heading of fertility data the European group regard 'duration of marriage' and 'whether the current marriage is the first marriage or not' as 'basic'; additional topics mentioned are 'year of birth of each person born alive to women in their first marriage', 'number of live-born children of current marriage which are not first marriages', and 'number of times married'. 'School attendance' becomes an 'additional' topic. The European list is more specific in referring to the family *nucleus* rather than to the family (see Section 9).

9. *Concepts and Definitions*

We may now consider the census topics in more detail especially in relation to their purpose and the underlying concepts which form the basis of the census questions. With regard to 'purpose' it may be remarked that there have been many developments in the application of census results in recent decades and most of them fall within the same broad direction of orientation, namely, the provision of more information about the social and economic characteristics of populations and about the pattern of social and economic organization of communities. The increasing emphasis upon economic aspects of population changes has been an out-standing feature of demographic study. In addition there have been new pressures at work. Growing interest in the social stresses of modern industrial development and con-comitant urbanization and the relationship between economic and social changes has led to intensified studies into these aspects of sociology, which in turn have brought demands for relevant statistical data.

9.1 HOUSING
To the census authority, dwellings and people are inseparable in the sense that it is difficult and very largely meaningless to measure housing resources without relating those resources to their present as well as their potential use. It is therefore customary in most countries to conduct the housing census

31

simultaneously with, and as an integral part of, the population census. On the one hand, this enables housing data to be classified in relation to the characteristics of the population accommodated in the dwelling units (as a means of assessing the adequacy of housing), and on the other hand, it makes it possible to classify the population in relation to their housing (as a means of measuring both current levels of living and potential housing demand).

There is a practical consideration too. The basic procedure of enumeration is to patrol a defined area of land, to identify buildings, to decide which of the buildings have people living in them and within these buildings to identify house-holds (whether there at the time or not) as the primary count-ing unit. In this procedure the identification of households is related to a defined housing unit. It is difficult in prac-tice therefore to carry out a population census without at the same time carrying out a large part of a housing census.

This does not preclude the carrying out of separate and more intensive surveys by housing or planning authorities for development purposes, especially where such surveys are concerned with structural conditions the assessment of which may be a technical matter beyond the competence of the population census authority. For example, in Great Britain the population census of 1966 which embraced considerable housing information was followed in 1967 by a 'National House Condition Survey' on a sample basis. Some 6000 dwellings in 250 local authority areas were inspected by Public Health or Building Surveyors, the object being to classify dwellings in the following categories:

(a) unfit dwellings likely to be dealt with under Part II of the Housing Act 1957 (broadly this refers to *individual* dwellings to be demolished or closed);

(b) unfit dwellings likely to be dealt with under Part III of the Housing Act 1957 (this refers to clearance *areas* constituted by two or more unfit dwellings);

(c) dwellings needing improvement, but not capable of it and also in need of excessive repair;

(d) dwellings needing improvement and capable of it;

(e) dwellings not needing improvement but in need of major repair;

(f) satisfactory dwellings

Analytical developments have taken the form of more detailed cross-tabulations between household structural groups and classifications of types of housing accommodation. It is now regarded as inadequate to classify housing units merely according to the number of rooms they contain. A number of new axes of classification have been introduced.

In the first place there has been some international standardization, as a result of United Nations guidance (Conference of European Statisticians 1968) in the classification of housing units. A housing unit is defined as 'a structurally separate and independent living place which by the way it has been built, rebuilt, converted or arranged, is designed for human habitation or, if not designed for human habitation, is actually used for this purpose at the time of the census'. Premises designed for human habitation which at the time of the census are used wholly for non-residential purposes are excluded as also are rustic, improvised, mobile and collective premises which are unoccupied at the time of the census.

A housing unit can be:

(a) an occupied or vacant house, apartment, room, or suite of rooms; or

(b) an occupied hut, cabin, shack, caravan, houseboat, hotel, institution, camp, etc.; or

(c) a barn, mill, cave or any other shelter used for human habitation at the time of the census.

A building may contain several housing units and a housing unit may, exceptionally be located in more than one building, for example, where a dwelling comprises a main building and room(s) above a detached garage that are clearly designed to be used as part of the dwelling. Several households may live together in a housing unit and, exceptionally, a single household may occupy more than one housing unit as its usual place of residence.

New housing units ought to be included when construction has been completed and they are ready for occupation. Housing units being demolished should be excluded, but occupied housing units and vacant dwellings awaiting demolition should be included. Dwellings which are vacant because they are undergoing repair or conversion should also be included.

The essential features of a housing unit are separateness and independence. An enclosure is *separate* if surrounded by walls, and covered by a roof so that a person or a group of persons, can isolate themselves from other persons in the community for the purposes of sleeping, preparing and taking meals or protecting themselves from the hazards of climate and environment. The housing unit is *independent* when it has direct access from the street or from a public or communal staircase, passage, gallery or grounds, that is, when the occupants can come in and go out of it without passing through anybody else's accommodation.

In the British census of 1966 the term 'dwelling' rather than housing unit was used and the instructions to enumerators contained the following:

Dwelling

For a unit of accommodation to count as a dwelling for census purposes it must satisfy certain specific requirements. Unless a clear and precise standard is imposed no one will know what the census housing statistics really mean. The broad basis of the census standard is that for accommodation to count as a dwelling it must give the occupants roughly the same degree of privacy that is available in an ordinary unconverted house or in a flat in a purpose-built block; the accommodation must be structurally separate behind its own front door and the occupants must be able to get in and out without passing through anyone else's living quarters.

So-called flats in large houses are not always dwellings from the census point of view. The following paragraphs show you how to determine whether or not accommodation counts as a dwelling.

The most usual situation is quite straightforward and is one of the following:

(i) The normal house (detached, semi-detached or terraced) which has not been altered in any way for occupation by more than one household.

(ii) A bungalow (detached or semi-detached).

(iii) A flat or maisonette in a purpose-built block of flats or maisonettes.

(iv) A flat which is the only living accommodation in premises otherwise used for non-residential purposes (shop, office, etc.).

(v) A caravan.

(vi) A chalet.

(vii) A houseboat.

Each of the above always counts as one dwelling no matter how many households may be living there.

The decision becomes more difficult when a house which was originally built as accommodation for one household has been altered to provide several units of accommodation. The alterations may be slight (the provision of another kitchen, for example); they may be major structural changes resulting in the complete re-designing of the interior lay-out; or they may be something in between.

If the alterations amount only to the provision of additional household amenities (bathroom, kitchen, washing-up place,

35

etc.), the whole house constitutes one dwelling and the so-called flats within it are merely household spaces in that dwelling.

If the alterations are such that all the flats in the converted building are structurally separate as is the case with flats in a purpose-built block, then each flat counts as a dwelling.

If, however, the conversion has been less thorough and not all of the flats are self-contained behind their own front doors (a bed-sitting-room, sometimes called a one-room flatlet, with shared use of a bathroom does not count as being self-contained) then each flat is merely a household space and the whole building counts as the dwelling. An exception to this rule occurs when part of the converted building has been permanently separated off from the rest (locked doors or doors blocked by furniture do not count as providing permanent separation) and has its own means of access from outside. In such circumstances the whole building constitutes two dwellings, the separated part being one and the remainder of the building the other.

The following examples illustrate the points made above.

FIRST EXAMPLE

Situation

Additional kitchens, bathrooms, etc., have been installed in a three-storey house so that these amenities are available on each floor, but no other structural alterations have been made.

Classification: The whole house is one dwelling.

SECOND EXAMPLE

Situation

A three-storey house has been converted into three flats, one on each floor. In each flat the whole of the accommodation is contained behind one door which opens on to the hall or landing.

Classification: Each of the three flats is a separate dwelling.

THIRD EXAMPLE

Situation

A three-storey house has been converted into three flats, one on each floor. In each of the lower two flats the whole of the accommodation is contained behind one door which opens on to the hall or landing. In the flat on the top floor there is no single 'front door' and all the rooms which make up the accommodation open on to the landing, enabling the occupants of the flat to use the landing when passing from one room to another.

Classification: Because of the situation on the top floor, none of the flats in the building can be classified as a dwelling. The whole house counts as one dwelling.

FOURTH EXAMPLE
Situation

A three-storey house with a basement has been converted into four flats. The original access from the basement to the ground floor has been bricked up and access from the basement to the street is provided by the original basement door. The flats on the other three floors are not self-contained behind their own 'front doors', but each have all their rooms opening on to the hall or landing.

Classification: the basement is a dwelling. But the other three flats do not count as such; they are merely household spaces in that part of the building which is above the basement, and the whole of that part counts as one dwelling.

FIFTH EXAMPLE
Situation

A three-storey house with a basement has been converted into four flats. The basement has an outside door and a door leading to the hall on the ground floor. The other flats are each self-contained behind a 'front door' which opens on to the hall or landing.

Classification: Each of the four flats (including the basement flat) is a separate dwelling. But if—
Situation

The flats on the ground floor and first floor are each self-contained behind their own 'front door', but the top-floor flat is not self-contained and has all its rooms opening on to the landing. Then—

Classification: The whole building, including the basement, is one dwelling.

Institutional premises

This term covers all establishments in which some form of communal catering is provided for the people in them, such as hotels, holiday camps, hospitals, religious communities, boarding-schools, prisons, H.M. Forces establishments, etc. (inns and hotels without sleeping accommodation for guests are not institutions but will often contain private households).

Married quarters in H.M. Forces establishments and dwellings for prison staff do not form part of the institution but in all other circumstances institutional premises comprise all the buildings, including any houses for resident staff, within the boundaries of the establishment. There may be separate private households and separate dwellings within these premises and the rules for identifying them are:

(i) a person or group of people in an institution can count as a separate household only if they are either – (*a*) a family which does not normally depend on the institution for the provision of meals, or (*b*) a person or group for whom the institution does not provide any daily meals; and

(ii) living quarters in an institution count as a separate dwelling, even though accessible only through the institution.

Do not identify separate dwellings in the grounds of an institution if they are occupied by people who do not constitute a private household. For example, a house which is being used as sleeping quarters for nurses counts as part of the hospital not as a separate dwelling.

There are for census purposes two categories of institution – 'large' institutions and 'smaller' institutions. The division is based mainly on the number of people who were present in these establishments at the 1961 census. The institutions in your district which are classified as 'large' are listed in your record book under the heading 'Large Institutions'. In these establishments one person in every ten will be selected for inclusion in the sample. (In hotels and similar places everyone will be enumerated and the sample chosen later at the census office. In other cases the person in charge of the institution will select the sample from a list of all those present on census night.) The 'smaller' institutions which have been selected for inclusion in the sample will be included among the sample addresses in your record book and in these cases everyone present must be enumerated. Whatever circumstances you may find at any particular institution you must not alter the size category to which it has already been allotted. For example, if a 'smaller' institution is discovered to have fifty residents it must not be added to your list of 'Large Institutions' but dealt with according to the rules for the 'smaller' category.

If you find that an establishment shown in your list of 'Large Institutions' has changed in character and is no longer an institution (for example, an hotel which has been converted into flats), enumerate everyone in the premises but on the basis of private households in private dwellings. Apply instructions 10 and 12 to discover how many households and dwellings there are.[1] If a sample address is an annexe to an institution which is on your list of 'Large Institutions', treat the annexe as part of the institution and note your record book to show when the annexe was acquired.

The enumerators were also required to code the type of building in which the dwelling was located as:

A. Any house or bungalow which constitutes a single dwelling; a houseboat.
B. A building which consists of non-residential or institutional premises plus a single dwelling (for example, a shop with one flat above).
C. A purpose-built block of flats or maisonettes.
D. A building which has been converted to provide more than one dwelling.
E. A caravan.

If a building with non-residential or institutional premises

---

[1] These instructions refer to the census definitions of 'household' and 'dwelling'.

had more than one dwelling associated with it (for example, a shop plus two dwellings) the enumerators were instructed to ignore the non-residential part and code the building C or D according to the relevant circumstances.

The purpose of such a classification of building structures is to throw light on the extent to which land shortage or public preference has drawn people to live in blocks of flats rather than in single dwellings. There are important social implications especially for families with children (questions of noise, play facilities, privacy) and old people (dangers of staircases, limitations of access). It would be useful to supplement the information by inquiring about the number of floors and the presence or absence of a lift. For planning purposes the classification may be further extended to cover, for example, period of construction, as indicators of obsolescence.

The international recommendation for the classification of housing units (United Nations 1967) is as follows:

1. *Housing Units*
    1.1 Conventional dwellings.
    1.2 Mobile housing units.
    1.3 Marginal housing units.
        1.3.1 Improvised housing units (makeshift shelters of various kinds).
        1.3.2 Units in permanent buildings not intended for human habitation (stables, barns, garages, etc.).
        1.3.3 Other premises not intended for human habitation (e.g. caves).

2. *Living quarters other than housing units*
    2.1 Hotels, rooming houses or other lodging houses (where number of boarders or lodgers exceeds five).
    2.2 Institutions (see below).
    2.3 Camps (essentially intended for *temporary* accom-

modation of groups with common interests or activities).

2.4 Living quarters not otherwise classifiable (e.g. a kibbutz in Israel).

The definition of an institution is a 'set of premises in a permanent structure or structures designed to house groups (usually large) of persons who are bound by either a common public objective or a common personal interest ... persons of the same sex frequently share dormitories'. Hospitals, military barracks, boarding-schools, convents, prisons, etc., fall within this category.'

The Conference of European Statisticians has not proposed any significant departure from this classification.

An important axis for cross-tabulation is the tenure as owner-occupier, tenant, or sub-tenant. This may be regarded as an economic characteristic of the household.

In the British population census of 1966 the following questions were asked of each head of household:

Does your household occupy its accommodation (house, flat, rooms, etc.)—

(*a*) As owner-occupier (including purchase by mortgage).

(*b*) By renting it with a farm, shop, or other business premises.

(*c*) By virtue of employment.

(*d*) By renting it from the Council or New Town Corporation or Commission.

(*e*) By renting it unfurnished from a private landlord or company.

(*f*) By renting it furnished from a private landlord or company.

(*g*) In some other way. Please give details.

Answer 'Yes' to only one of the questions (*a*), (*b*), (*c*), (*d*), (*e*) or (*f*) or give details at (*g*).

The notes to the question stated that 'If the house, flat, etc., is occupied on a lease which was originally granted for at least twenty-one years or has since been extended to twenty-one years or more write 'Yes' at (*a*). For shorter leases answer one of the other parts.

If the accommodation is provided in connection with the employment of a member of your household and ceases to be provided after the employment comes to an end (e.g. tied cottage, caretaker's flat) write 'Yes' at (*c*) whether rent is paid or not.

The information under (*g*) was subsequently assigned to codes by the census staff. The reply, 'Provided by employer', or a 'house provided to clergyman or minister of religion, e.g. rectory, vicarage, manse, etc.' were assigned to (*c*). The replies 'grace and favour residence', 'owned by relative, no rent paid', 'unfurnished almshouse', 'rented from employer (independently of occupation)', 'rented from previous employer', 'retired, house provided rent free by previous employer' were assigned to (*e*). The replies 'owned and furnished by a relative, no rent paid', 'almshouse, furnished' were assigned to (*f*).

The main characteristics of the housing unit to be tabulated within the type-groups discussed above are:

(i) Size, i.e. number of rooms.
(ii) Number of occupying households, and persons.
(iii) Facilities (water supply, toilet, bath, ventilation, etc.).
(iv) Tenure.
(v) Social and economic characteristics of head of household.

Commonly (i) and (ii) are crossed (to give density for each household size) within each housing unit. There is also a need to examine the housing of special sections of the population (for example, old people living alone or certain specified household structures); estimates of the adequacy or inadequacy of the existing stock of housing on various hypotheses as to the space needs of different household (and family) structures: studies of the sharing of dwellings in terms of the structural types of household which combine to share; studies of obsolescence (as indicated by lack of facilities or evidence of conversion from original design). Household composition is therefore a further important axis of classification.

The concept of household structure as such is dealt with later. The other axes of classification give rise to practical difficulties which we must consider.

9.2 ROOMS

The count of rooms always causes difficulty. The 1966 Census in Great Britain in asking for the number of rooms occupied by the household said, 'Include all living-rooms, bedrooms and kitchens whether or not at present in use. Include a scullery if it is used for cooking. Do not include a bathroom, toilet, closet, landing, lobby or recess; a scullery which is not used for cooking; a storeroom, office, shop or any other room which is used solely for business purposes. A large room which can be divided by a sliding or folding fixed partition should count as two rooms. A room which is divided by curtains or portable screens into separate sections (e.g. for living and sleeping) should count as one room.

Prefabricated extensions should also count as rooms if regularly used for living, eating, sleeping or cooking.'

The question asked was:

(a) How many rooms are there in your accommodation ———
(b) How many of these rooms are a kitchen or scullery ———
(c) How many of the kitchens or sculleries shown at (b) are regularly used for breakfast or any other meal ———

In ordinary unshared dwellings the head of the household completed the answers to this question, but in shared dwellings the enumerator completed them for each householder. The enumerator also provided an estimate of the number of rooms in vacant accommodation and in accommodation from which the occupier was absent at the time of the census. Where the households in shared dwellings shared the use of any room it was credited to one household to avoid the use of fractions in the tabulations. Questions (b) and (c) were included because whereas in 1966 a 'room' included all kitchens, in 1961 kitchens were only counted if used regularly for meals and it was desired to compare 1966 with 1961 on the 1961 basis.

Although these definitions were drafted with care there nevertheless remains an inherent element of subjectivity in the response. 'Regularly used for living.' The term 'regularly' is difficult enough but the term 'living' can obviously cover a very wide range of activity. If you stand in a cubicle (e.g. to put articles away) is it being used for living? Doubtless it would be possible to establish criteria to inject a greater degree of objectivity but this would impose an amount of complexity and tedium on householder and enumerator alike that might jeopardize response to the census as a whole. Most census authorities rely on common sense and accept the inherent errors of response. For the greater part of the population the response is straightforward and consistent (on successive occasions) even if it does not always accord with the interpretation which the census authority would impose; for most people boxrooms and other rooms which are in doubt as to the potential for 'living' in do not exist or are randomly ignored or counted. Most difficulty arises in some snobbish households where on the one hand they wish to inflate the number of rooms they possess and yet on the other would be very reluctant to admit to eating breakfast in the kitchen; and in a minority of more informed people who want to 'correct' the definitions given by the census authority. The latter group find difficulty with almost every census question.

They mean well and are often very reasonable; they cannot however appreciate that the refinements which they consider necessary are quite impossible to apply on a massive scale; nor can they appreciate that the man-in-the-street leads a far less complicated life and is not troubled by the distinctions between the different situations which they recognize.

There is one general truth that is worth stressing at this point. It applies to most of the concepts and definitions used in the population census. It is this. If the census authority in respect of any piece of information (like a 'room' or a 'household', etc.) uses a concept which is different from that normally accepted by the public, then no matter how often repeated or how boldly printed, it will largely be ignored; the public will substitute the concept with which they are more familiar. If it were to be publicly accepted that a bathroom is a living-room then it would be so counted despite exhortation to the contrary. Certainly if the census authority wishes to rely on common sense it must use commonly accepted definitions. If this is not what is required for census purposes then a further question must be asked to enable the semantic gap to be bridged. For example, if it were desired to exclude from living-rooms a type of room which the public regarded as a living-room, then the number of this type must be asked for so that the census authority can make its own exclusion.

A post-enumeration survey carried out after the 1961 census in Great Britain (General Register Office 1968) indicated an overstatement in numbers of rooms of just over one-half per cent. A substantial part of this error in the number of rooms arose from kitchens. (In 1961 a kitchen should have been counted only if used for eating.) Overstatement occurred because kitchens were claimed as rooms though they were not used for eating, and understatement occurred because they were sometimes not so claimed when meals were eaten in them. If the stated kitchen element is removed the net overstatement of rooms reduces from 59 per 10,000 to about 20 per 10,000, a very low level of error. In 1966, kitchens were included in the gross total and a separate question was asked about kitchens used for meals; it is likely that accuracy was even more closely approached.

9.3 HOUSEHOLD AMENITIES

While the assessment of the current stock of housing tends to focus first upon the balance or imbalance of (*a*) numbers of dwellings and numbers of households and (*b*) the size distribution (in rooms) of dwellings and the size distribution (in persons) of households, there are other considerations. First, two households of the same size may require different accommodation because their composition is different. (A married couple will normally share a bedroom; the unmarried will do so only if they are of the same sex or if not are very young.) We will look at this later. Second, there is a question of the condition of the dwelling. As already indicated there is a limit to what may be asked at a population census but it is feasible to ask about the presence or absence of well-defined amenities, as indicating the need for measures of improvement. The question on this subject in the 1966 census of Great Britain was as follows:

In the following questions—

a hot water tap means a tap within the building and connected to any form of heating appliance (e.g. boiler, tank with immersion heater, geyser, etc.) which in turn is connected to a piped water supply;

a water-closet means a flush toilet emptying into a main sewer, septic tank or cesspool. It does not include a chemical closet or earth closet;

a fixed bath means a bath permanently connected to a

water supply and with a wastepipe leading outside the building;

a fixed shower means a shower permanently connected to a water supply and with a waterpipe leading outside the building;

(a) Has your household the use of a hot water tap within the building? Write 'yes' or 'no' _____

(b) If 'yes' is it shared with another household? Write yes or 'no' _____

(c) Has your household the use of a water-closet (W.C.) with entrance inside the building? Write 'yes' or 'no' _____

(d) If 'yes' is it shared with another household? Write 'yes' or 'no' _____

(e) Has your household the use of a water-closet (W.C.) with entrance outside the building (e.g. in the garden, backyard or lane)? Write 'yes' or 'no' _____

(f) If 'yes' is it shared with another household? Write 'yes' or 'no' _____

(g) Has your household the use of a fixed bath within the building? Write 'yes' or 'no' _____

(h) If 'yes' is it shared with another household? Write 'yes' or 'no' _____

(i) Has your household the use of a fixed shower within the building? Write 'yes' or 'no' _____

In 1961 a water-closet was defined as one within or 'attached' to the building. Since the water-closet attached to a building could be accessible from either inside or outside the building the coverage was quite different from that of (c) above, or even of (c) and (e) taken together. In fact the 1961 post-enumeration survey showed that the question in the form then used had been widely misunderstood. Water-closets near to but not physically attached to the building were included while on the other hand a number of households with use of a water-closet within the census definition stated that they had no use of a water-closet. On balance 'sole use' was overstated by 3 per cent of the true figure and 'shared' by 8 per cent, while 'none' was understated by 60 per cent of the true figure. (Some of this error was removed from the published tables by editing procedures – see later.)

This is another example of the effect of a difference between a concept (i.e. 'attached') which the census authority attempted to impose, and that which was commonly acceptable to the public. To most people a water-closet in the garden of a house (and constructed as part of the amenities of the house) was 'attached' to it even though physically separated by several yards. If a pilot census had been permitted prior to the 1961 Census (as it was before the 1966 Census) this difficulty would have immediately emerged and the census question would have been appropriately rephrased.

9.4 CARS AND GARAGING

Partly because a garage is an additional housing amenity and partly because the traffic authorities need to measure changes in the ownership of cars and the facilities for garaging (whether on or off street), a new question was introduced at the 1966 Census of Great Britain, as follows:

Car and garaging

(*a*) How many cars, including vans, taxed wholly or in part as private vehicles are owned or used exclusively by you and members of your household (see notes below). If none, write 'none'   ——

Notes

Include cars or vans provided or subsidized by members' employers for business or pleasure and used exclusively by members of your household.

Do not include—

Cars or vans taxed wholly as goods vehicles or hackney carriages; cars or vans owned by members of your household but not used by any member of your household; cars or vans belonging to visitors.

(b) For each car or van entered at (a) show where it is normally kept overnight by writing 'yes' at (i), (ii), (iii) or (iv) or by giving details at (v). If there are more than two vehicles give answers for only two of them.

	1st vehicle	2nd vehicle	code
(i) In a garage or carport within the grounds of your dwelling	———	———	1
(ii) In a garage or carport elsewhere	———	———	2
(iii) Within the grounds of your dwelling but not in a garage or carport	———	———	3
(iv) On the road, street or verge	———	———	4
(v) Elsewhere – please give details	———————		5

Information on garaging was collected for up to two cars per household. The garaging arrangements for a third and subsequent cars was regarded as 'not stated' and given code 6.

The full evaluation of the results of the census has not yet been published but little difficulty seems to have been experienced in the application of the definitions used in the question.

9.5 NAME

We turn now to personal and household characteristics as distinct from dwelling characteristics. Names of persons in the household are not important census data in ultimate usage but they serve important intermediate purposes. That part of the census schedule for Great Britain which provides for the listing of the characteristics of individual members of the household always asks that for each person the particulars commence with

> ... names and surnames of each person to be included; begin with the head of the household, then relatives, visitors, boarders, etc. Babies should be included. If they have not been given a name write 'baby' and the surname. Do this before going on to the next question.

Asking the householder to list names in a systematic order does help him to ensure completeness. He can refer to the list of names and so satisfy himself that he has accounted for everybody present on census night. The reference to babies is important because infants especially if unnamed have always been overlooked in some instances and therefore underenumerated. At the data processing stage especially when the schedules are being validated prior to coding, reference to names helps in cases of doubt to decide whether, in fact, one household or more than one household is included and whether, for example, relationship to head of household and marital condition are correctly recorded. Names are also important for subsequent identification of the person to whom a particular set of census characteristics relate – either for the purposes of reference back in the event of incompleteness or inadequacy of those particulars or for the purpose of confirming relationships (blood, marital, or dependency) in the coding of household composition.

9.6 MEMBERSHIP OF HOUSEHOLDS

The question that immediately now arises is 'Who are the persons to be listed on the census schedule?' The schedule in Great Britain and in most other countries, is a *household* document to be completed by the head of the household (see later as to definition). In Great Britain in 1961 and in preceding censuses the main count was on a de facto basis, i.e. of persons actually in the household at the time of the census whether or not they were normally members of the household. The notice of the schedule stated, 'The head, or person acting as head, of a private household is recognized by law to make a return in this form in respect of all persons (members of the household, including visitors, employees and boarders) who are present at midnight on the night of Sunday, 23 April 1961, in the dwelling and all persons who arrive at the dwelling and join the household on Monday, 24 April 1961, before the collection of the schedule, and who have not been enumerated elsewhere.' Such a definition leads to population for areal units (for example local authority areas) which are also on a de facto basis (as distinct from a de jure basis, i.e. allocating population to the area to which they naturally belong and whose authority they recognize as governing them).

The 10 per cent sample schedule of the 1961 census did provide for the reconstitution of the de jure household in that Part III of the schedule, entitled 'persons absent from this household' called for the listing of particulars 'of all persons usually living in this household who are absent on census night, except those arriving next day who have been included in Part I'. It was considered at the time that for housing purposes it was important that, if only on a sample basis, local authorities should be able to compare the size distribution of households on both a de facto and a de jure basis. It was also essential that the de jure household should be identified for the analysis of household structures. Such an analysis (for example of the ratio of earners to non-earners, or of the presence or absence of ancestors of the family nucleus) might be misleading if it were not based on households as normally constituted.

Similar provision was made in the 1966 sample census in Great Britain. At this census, heads of private households were instructed to give particulars for:

(1) Each person alive at midnight on 24 April 1966 who spends

51

Sunday night 24/25 April 1966 (census night) in this household, and

(2) Each person who usually lives in this household but spends census night elsewhere, and

(3) Each person who arrives in this household next day (Monday) before noon and who has spent the night travelling.

The following additional instructions were given in notes accompanying the schedule:

Persons to be included:

(i) Everyone who usually lives in the household must be included on the census form whether they are present or absent on census night, 24/25 April.

(ii) Visitors spending census night in the household should be included, also those who arrive on Monday morning (25 April) having spent census night travelling.

(iii) Do not include any absent family member who usually lives at another address (for example, a son who has left home and is living in lodgings or a person living permanently in an institution such as an old people's home or who has lived there for the past six months).

Nevertheless the published *enumerated populations* were defined as *excluding* absent members of private households. For population count purposes the traditional de facto basis was retained. Information about absent members was used only for analysis of household structure for which a de jure basis was essential.

The terms 'present' and 'absent' were defined in the following way:

(i) Write 'present' for all people who spend census night here. Members of the household who are out on night work should also be marked 'present'. So should anyone who arrives before midday on Monday having spent census night travelling.

(ii) Write 'absent' only for household members who are spending census night away from home (other than on night work). For example, write 'absent' for a schoolboy who lives at home during the holidays but is now away at boarding-school or for anyone temporarily away on his job, on holiday or in hospital (including a new-born baby).

(iii) For people marked 'absent' write also the full postal address of the place where they are staying on Census night. If the precise address is not known write the name of the town or village where the person is staying. For anyone temporarily absent abroad write the name of the country.

Instruction (iii) served to help the householder to test whether or not the person was absent, i.e. was in fact at another address; it also served to assist the census authority to check, in cases of doubt, whether the person was enumerated at the address at which they were alleged to be on census night. Experience gained in the 1961 Census suggested that even where a de facto basis is to be adopted for the main enumeration it is important to provide, on all schedules, for absent members to be listed as such (with their actual location at the time of the census) otherwise the householder may be inclined to include them as de facto members of the household. The 1966 instructions evidently take account of this instruction.

9.7 HOUSEHOLD AND FAMILY COMPOSITION

The population census is concerned not only with 'counting heads' but with identifying the family and household groupings, i.e. the way in which individual people combine together to satisfy their living needs. This is clearly an essential requirement for understanding the social and economic conditions of the people; it is a part of those social and economic conditions, it is a part of the mechanism by which the total national product is created, distributed and consumed. A knowledge of the life cycle of the growth and disruption of families is necessary for the proper understanding of population growth and for the assessment of consumer demand for almost all commodities and especially for estimating housing needs.

The concept of the family is easy to grasp because of its primary biological significance; that of the household, with its economic rather than biological content, is more difficult to define. Because there has been some confusion about both concepts, the Working Group on Census of Population and Housing of the E.C.E. Conference of European Statisticians has recommended the following definitions:

A private household[1] may be:

(a) a one-person household, viz. a person who lives alone in a separate housing unit (as already defined) or who occupies, as a lodger, a part or the whole of a separate room or rooms in a part of a housing unit but does not join together with any of the other occupants of the housing unit to form part of a multi-person household as defined below; or

(b) a multi-person household, defined as a group of two or more persons who combine together jointly to occupy the whole or part of a housing unit, and to provide themselves with food *or* other essentials for living. The group may pool their incomes and have a common budget to a greater or lesser extent in different circumstances. The group may be composed of related persons or unrelated persons or a combination of both, including boarders but excluding lodgers. (*Boarders* take meals with the private household and generally are allowed to use all the available household facilities. *Lodgers* however are sub-tenants who have hired part of the housing unit for their exclusive use. They may

---

[1] A collective or institutional household is separately defined as comprising persons 'living in hotels, boarding-houses, colleges, schools, hospitals, military installations, penal establishments', who are subject to a common authority or are bound by a common objective and/or personal interests and characteristics.

or may not have meals regularly with the household but they are distinguished from boarders principally by the fact that they do not automatically enjoy the use of all available household facilities.)

The basic criteria under this concept of household, which for the sake of convenience may be referred to as the housekeeping unit concept, are that the persons constituting the household jointly occupy a common dwelling space, that they share principal meals (unless prevented for example by working conditions), and that they make common provision for basic living needs (such as lighting, heating, laundry, etc.). Thus, a multi-person household may be comprised of the members of a family and relatives, resident domestic servants, employees and other persons living with the family as a single housekeeping unit whether or not this group occupies the whole or only a part of a structurally separate dwelling. (It is implicit for this concept that members of the household temporarily absent on census night should be brought within its scope, i.e. we are concerned here with the de jure household.)

In the population census it is possible within households to identify families defined as persons who are related by blood, marriage, or adoption. In this definition the marriage relationship includes stable de facto unions. The broad concept is of a group or groups of related persons found to be living together within a household. In many cases the family and the household will be identical. There may be different specific concepts according to the object of the statistical analysis. For example, it may be desirable for some purposes to consider:

(a) The family in the narrow sense, limited to a married couple with one or more unmarried children, a married couple without children, or one parent with one or more unmarried children, each of which may be called a 'family nucleus'.

(b) The family comprising all the related members of a household.

(c) Family relationships extending beyond the household are sometimes considered for sociological or genetic purposes, but this concept of the entire biological family is not suitable for census purposes.

For census purposes the primary unit is the family nucleus because it is the unit which most facilitates analysis of family and household structure.

It is important to bear in mind that there is a clear methodological distinction between the household and the family (as defined above). The household is identified by the census enumerator; the family, as such, is not identified by the enumerator but is fixed mechanically during the data processing on the basis of information written into the census schedule in respect of all members of the household. It is therefore more natural to proceed from households to families. It will also be important to bear in mind that a classification of households will to some extent involve a classification of family components of households.

The head of the household is usually considered in the conduct of the census to be that person who is acknowledged as such by the other household members. It is more important for purposes of household composition and dependency statistics, however, to identify the person on whom falls the chief responsibility for the economic maintenance of the household, i.e. the main breadwinner or the principal contributor to the household budget, who may be called the 'main supporter'. The identification requires either a direct question in the census schedule or the establishment of criteria, e.g. economic activity, socio-economic category, sex, seniority of age, etc., by means of which a choice is made during the data-processing.

The same approach can also be made in relation to the

family nucleus. This gives rise to the concepts of the head of the family nucleus and the supporter of such a family. Often these persons are identical; and when the household comprises only one family nucleus, the analysis of the household coincides with that of the family.

Households may be classified first according to whether they constitute private or institutional households. Private households can then be classified into non-family, one-family, and multi-family households (the latter may be further sub-divided according to the number of family nuclei they contain). Non-family households may be classified into one-person and multi-person households; the multi-person households may be further subdivided into those consisting of related persons only, of related and unrelated persons, and of unrelated persons only. Distinction could also be made between direct descent and other relationship (e.g. between a grandfather and a grandchild on the one hand and two sisters on the other). One-family households may be classified into the following types:

(a) A married couple with one or more unmarried children
(b) A married couple without children
(c) One parent with one or more unmarried children.

Each of these types of family nucleus may be combined with other persons either related, unrelated, or both within the household. Multi-family households are classified according to whether or not any of the family nuclei are related and whether or not this relationship is in direct descent; in addition, the family nuclei themselves may be classified by type as already indicated for those in one-family households. The number of possible combinations of axes of classification is therefore large, and it has been suggested that though full analysis may have to be undertaken on occasions, for most practical purposes the analysis of households (as distinct from families) would be facilitated if each multi-family household could be typified by a primary family within it. This primary family could be selected on the basis of criteria related to the object of the analysis. For example, it could be the family nucleus with the oldest head, or the family nucleus containing the main economic supporter of the household, etc. The breakdown of a large household in accordance with the principles outlined above is shown in Table I on p. 60.

The analysis of families is best undertaken in terms of family nuclei. Just as in household analysis the development is from households to the family nuclei of which they are composed and which serve to differentiate the households, so it is necessary in family analysis to proceed from different types of family nuclei to their disposition within the households into which they are integrated. For completeness, it should be borne in mind that family nuclei living as members of institutional households have to be included. Thus, in the first place, it is necessary to identify the three types of family nuclei, living in both private and institutional households. Secondly, the family nuclei living in private households are classified according to whether they are in one-family, two-family, three-family, etc., households. Where for the purpose of household analysis certain family nuclei have been designated as primary families and the others as secondary families, this designation provides a further axis of classification.

These household classifications are relatively simple and capable of further development, as indeed has been the case in some countries, notably in the Federal Republic of Germany, where they have introduced the interesting concept of the 'functional scope of households', i.e. for each individual the extent to which he participates in the basic functions of the household, for example, by:

(a) Sharing meals which are prepared for the household in common.

(b) Having laundry washed together with that of the total household.

(c) Contributing to a common budget from which the requirements of daily life are financed.

This clearly provides a further measure of the cohesion of households and an additional axis of classification.

Cross-tabulations from the basic distribution of household or family types would show for each type the number of persons in the household, the number and ages of children, and the number of earners and income recipients.

Another type of analysis that has been developed involves classifying households by the social and economic characteristics of a principal member, e.g. the chief economic supporter of the household. The characteristics cover a wide range and include occupancy of dwelling (as owner or tenants), level of education, type of activity, occupation, branch of economic activity, employment status, socio-economic group, as well as sex, age, and marital status.

It will be noted that the definition of household used in the census of Great Britain conforms to international recommendations and is based on the housekeeping concept. It has to be left to the enumerator to identify households and persons who are willing to accept responsibility as 'head of the household' for the completion of the census schedule. This is not always easy especially where two or more households are sharing a household unit.

The handbook issued to enumerators for the 1966 census set out the definition of a household and added:

A household will usually consist of the normal family living and eating together, but household and family are not necessarily one and the same as the following examples show:

59

TABLE I

A Three-Family Household

No.	Name	Relationship to Head	Sex Age	Marital condition	Occupation	Chief economic supporter	
						House-hold	Family
1.	Henry Brown	Head*	M.65	Married	Retired Farmer		
2.	Emily Brown	Spouse	F.60	Married	Housewife		
3.	George Brown	Son	M.42	Single	Farm Mng.	X	X
4.	Helen Brown	Daughter	F.39	Single	House duties	————	
5.	John Smith	Brother-in-law	M.62	Single	Carpenter (non-agric.)		
6.	James Robinson	Employee	M.60	Single	Farm worker	————	
7.	Eric Brown	Son	M.40	Married	Welder (non-agric.)		X
8.	Joan Brown	Daughter-in-law	F.38	Married	Housewife		
9.	David Brown	Grandson	M.10	—	—	————	
10.	Jane Jones	Sister-in-law	F.50	Widow	Family worker (farm)		X
11.	Mary Jones	Niece-in-law	F.30	Single	Teacher		

* Head in the conventional sense of accepting responsibility for the census schedule

Primary family nucleus: (1 + 2 + 3 + 4)

   (Note that 5 and 6 though related and unrelated respectively are not part of the family)

Secondary family nuclei: (7 + 8 + 9) in direct descent and (10 + 11) not in direct descent

Dependent on agriculture: economically inactive (1 + 2 + 4); economically active (3 + 6 + 10)

Dependent on other industry: economically inactive (8 + 9); economically active (5 + 7 + 11).

60

SITUATION	NUMBER OF HOUSEHOLDS
A Mr and Mrs Jones live in the same house as Mrs Jones's parents	One household if both families share a common housekeeping
	BUT
	Two households if each family caters for itself
B Miss Smith has a bed-sitting-room in a house occupied by Mr and Mrs White	One household if Miss Smith usually has at least one meal per day (breakfast counts as a meal) with the White family
	BUT
	Two households if Miss Smith is responsible for all her own catering

No guidance is given as to the identification of the head of the household as this, in Great Britain, is left to the household to decide for itself. The E.C.E. working party on population censuses has provided an algorithm for the identification of the head of household, in cases of doubt, as follows:

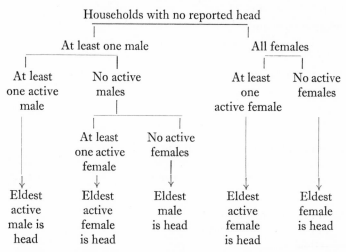

If it is decided to relate the structure of the household to the chief economic supporter then, in the absence of a positive statement from the household (and it has not hitherto been considered an acceptable census question), a slightly different procedure would be necessary. The computer algorithm adopted in the 1961 Census of Great Britain was as follows:

(i) Eliminate all visitors, boarders, and employees, children under 15 and all persons unrelated to the stated 'head of household'.

(ii) If any person on the household schedule is occupied, eliminate all persons not occupied; if no person is occupied but one is retired, eliminate all other unoccupied persons.

(iii) If any person remaining is the head of a family nucleus, i.e. accompanied by a wife and/or unmarried child(ren), eliminate all persons not heads of family nuclei.

(iv) If any person remaining is male, eliminate all females.

(v) Take the oldest person remaining; if two are of the same age, take the one entered first.

These rules were applied in turn to the persons in this household.

In the census of 1966 a more sophisticated system of scoring was applied, the person with the highest score being selected. Children under 15 and members of the household not related to the head were excluded from the scoring. The system was as below, the numbers shown representing the scores.

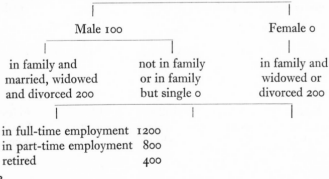

In the event of a tie, the eldest is selected (or if the ages are also equal, the first person on the schedule).

In the 1961 Census of Great Britain the analysis of household composition was made only for those households included in the 10 per cent sample receiving the schedule with the full range of census questions.[1] All members of a single household appeared on one schedule (columns being provided for answers to the various census questions on sex, age, occupation, etc.) and the relationship of each person to the nominal 'head' (not necessarily the chief economic supporter) was recorded in the manner indicated in Table I. The following relationships were given a numerical code.

Simple household consisting only of family nucleus (no other coding necessary).

Head of household.

Married child of Head (with separate indication of first, second, etc., if more than one).

Parent of Head (or Head's spouse).

Parent of Head's spouse, when parent of Head also present.

Grandparents or great-grandparents of Head.

Grandchildren of Head (single, unaccompanied by parents).

Married grandchild of Head (first, second, etc.).

Single sibling (without parent).

Married sibling (first, second, etc.).

Other relatives (not forming part of a family).

Other related families (first, second, etc.).

Domestic servants (not forming part of a family).

Families including one or more domestic servants (first, second, etc.).

Boarders not forming part of a family.

Families of Boarders (first, second, etc.).

Other persons, not forming part of a family.

---

[1] The remaining 90 per cent of households received a shorter schedule with very few questions.

Families of residents other than above (first, second, etc.).
Visitors not forming part of a family.
Families of visitors (first, second, etc.).

This list was comparatively short because the onus of recognizing families was placed on the coder and the code was applied to heads of families and to persons not in families; other members of families are given the code applicable to the head of their family. More than three-quarters of households contained no persons other than the head, spouse, and unmarried children. These were simple households consisting of one family nucleus only and were identified by a special mark on the first card only for each schedule. Thus for one million or so households (in the sample) it was necessary to make only one mark and to turn over two cards or so without marking them. The remaining million and a half cards required at least one mark each.

The recording of relationship to head was not entirely error-free. The terms 'lodger' and 'subtenant' occasionally appeared. If these terms were correct the person concerned should have formed separate households. There was also confusion between visitors and boarders. It was necessary in cases of doubt for coders to make subjective judgements on the basis of other information on the census schedule.

The computer then identified the type of household structure. The following classification was employed:

Household Type

$\left[\right]$ indicates alternative classification.

Domestic servants (including domestic servants' families) may occur in any class except o (*a*) without affecting the classification.

Domestic servant $=$ a domestic servant by 'relationship to head'.

Domestic servant family = a family of which the oldest economically active member or his/her spouse is a domestic servant.

Child = never-married child, or never-married grandchild without parent (great-grandchild without parent or grandparent).

Lone ancestor = ancestor (not in family) of head('s spouse) or of head's descendant('s spouse).

---

o. No family   (*a*) 1-person hh.   (i) no domestic servants.

                                                    (ii) with domestic servants.

                 (*b*) related, direct descent, with or without others.

                 (*c*) related, not direct descent.   (i) alone.

                                                    (ii) with unrelated.

                 (*d*) unrelated only.

1. One family   (*a*) married couple only.
                 (*b*) parent(s) with child(ren) only.
                 (*c*) (*a*) or (*b*) with lone ancestor(s) only.
                 (*d*) (*a*) to (*c*) with other relatives.
                 (*e*) (*a*) to (*d*) with unrelated.

                         (*m*) married couple without children, with or without others.

(*a*) to (*e*)   (*n*) married couple with child(ren), with or without others.

                         (*o*) lone parent with child(ren), with or without others.

(*b*) to (*e*)   (*p*) without lone ancestor(s), with or without others.

                         (*q*) with lone ancestor(s), with or without others.

2. Two   (*a*) direct   (*a*) without children of 2nd
families   descent   genern., no others.
                                  (ii) with children of 2nd genern.,
                                       no others.
                                 (iii) (i) or (ii) with others.

$$\begin{bmatrix} (r) \text{ (i) to (iii) without lone an-} \\ \text{cestor(s).} \\ (s) \text{ (iii) with lone ancestor(s).} \end{bmatrix}$$

           (*b*) not direct   (i) neither with children nor others.
               descent   (ii) one or both with children, no
                                     others.
                                 (iii) (i) or (ii) with others.

$$\begin{bmatrix} (t) \text{ (i) to (iii) without lone ances-} \\ \text{tor(s).} \\ (u) \text{ (iii) with lone ancestor(s).} \end{bmatrix}$$

3. Three or   (*a*) all direct   (i) without children of 2nd or
more   descent   higher genern., no others.
families   (ii) with child(ren) of 2nd or
                                     higher genern., no others.
                                 (iii) (i) or (ii) with others.

$$\begin{bmatrix} (v) \text{ (i) to (iii) without lone ances-} \\ \text{tor(s).} \\ (w) \text{ (iii) with lone ancestor(s).} \end{bmatrix}$$

           (*b*) not all   all
               direct
               descent

$$\begin{bmatrix} (x) \text{ without lone ancestor(s).} \\ (y) \text{ with lone ancestor(s).} \end{bmatrix}$$

$$\begin{bmatrix} 4. \ (a) \ 1. \text{ Married couple.} \\ 2. \text{ Parent and child.} \\ 3. \text{ Other relatives.} \\ 4. \text{ Unrelated.} \\ (b) \ 1. \text{ Father and son.} \\ 2. \text{ Father and daughter.} \\ 3. \text{ Mother and son.} \\ 4. \text{ Mother and daughter.} \\ (c) \ 0, 1, 2, 3 \text{ of main classification.} \end{bmatrix}$$

Possible alternative groupings were :

No. of groups

24	=	All except p to y
21	=	All except m to y
20	=	All except o (a) (i)
16	=	o entire
		All others except m to y
14	=	o (a) (i)
		(b)
		(a) (ii), (c), (d)
	1	(a)
		(p)
		(q)
	2	(a) (r)
		(s)
		(b) (t)
		(u)
	3	(a) (v)
		(w)
		(b) (x)
		(y)
8	=	o (a) (i)
		(b) (c)
		(a) (ii), (d)
	1	(m)
		(n)
		(o)
	2	(a), 3 (a)
	2	(b), 3 (b)

*Number of groups
identified*

22 All chief economic supporters by sex by

$$45, \ 45-\begin{Bmatrix} M\ 64 \\ F\ \ 59 \end{Bmatrix}, \ \begin{Bmatrix} M\ 65+ \\ F\ 60+ \end{Bmatrix} \tag{6}$$

Chief economic supporters who are family heads by
family type (10)

Chief economic supporters who are not family heads
by sex/age as for all chief economic supporters. (6)

10   1. Married couple with husband aged < 45
      2. Married couple with husband aged   45–64
      3. Married couple with husband aged   65+
      4. Married, spouse absent
      5. Single, widowed or divorced man aged   < 45
      6. Single, widowed or divorced man aged   45–64
      7. Single, widowed or divorced man aged   65+
      8. Single, widowed or divorced woman aged < 45
      9. Single, widowed or divorced woman aged   45–59
     10. Single, widowed or divorced woman aged   60+

4   Married couple with husband aged < 45, 45–64, 65+;
    lone parent.

2   Married couple, lone parent.

The 1966 tabulations have not yet been issued but preliminary indications are that the basic classifications used for household and families were not substantially different from those used in 1961.

An important development in the 1951 census of Great Britain and one which was extended in 1961 was the use of household classification in the preparation of estimates of housing (i.e. room) requirements according to various hypothetical standards of accommodation and the comparison of these estimates with the accommodation actually enjoyed by the different groups of households at the time of the census. The hypothesis used in 1961 census were:

I One living-room per household and a bedroom for each of its members, except that,
   (*a*) married couples identified should share a bedroom,
   (*b*) one but not more than one child under 5 should share the bedroom of its parents or of the head of the household.
   (*c*) In each family (including domestic servants' families),
      (i) up to three children under 5 should share a bedroom,
      (ii) one child under 5 and one 5 or over, of the same or opposite sex should share a bedroom,

(iii) two children aged 5 or over of the same sex should share a bedroom.

(d) All domestic servants of the same sex outside families should share one bedroom.

II Two living-rooms per household and a bedroom allocation the same as in I except that,

(a) no child shares a bedroom with its parent or the head of the household,

(b) up to two (not three) children under 5 should share a bedroom.

III As II except that for a one-person household there is only one living-room.

IV Two living-rooms per household and a bedroom for each of its members, except that

(a) married couples identified should share a bedroom,

(b) In each family (including domestic servants' families),

(i) up to two children under 11 should share a bedroom,

(ii) one child under 11 and one child over 11, of the same sex should share a bedroom,

(iii) two children over 11 of the same sex should share a bedroom.

Such tabulations bring out much more clearly the principal elements in the general imbalance between household size and dwelling size distributions; it enables one to see whether it is to a particular household structure, e.g. small households of one or two persons, that the imbalance might be attributed. Cross tabulation with tenure (owning or renting, etc.), and socio-economic group fill out the picture by indicating the relationship of housing inadequacy to social and economic conditions, it also suggests, by the extent to which the better circumstanced may be inadequately housed (i.e. crowding or sharing of dwelling by two families), the latent economic pressure for better housing should this become available by urban development.

The utility of this material is not limited to the formulation of housing policy. It is possible to tabulate for the different household types both numbers of children and numbers of earners (economically active); it is further possible to tabulate this information within each household type, according to the socio-economic group of the chief economic supporter. This gives an indication of the number of households at different levels of economic strength and of the numbers of children with different social and economic backgrounds, matters of some importance to those concerned with the social services and with education. If the tabulations are also made according to the industry of the chief economic supporter a measure is obtained of the extent to which groups of households are dependent upon particular industries. It is also possible to use the analysis of family composition to link information about the husband with that of the wife; for example, the socio-economic group of the husband can be cross-tabulated with that of the wife.

It is important to stress that these analyses are *derived* tabulations; they represent not the answers to direct but complicated questions on the schedule about household composition but the bringing together of answers to simpler questions about sex, age, family relationships, occupations, etc., which would have to be asked for other purposes. The burden is placed upon the data processing rather than on the public.

9.8. AGE, SEX

Errors in age statements are likely to be substantial in the early development of census taking especially where there is illiteracy and a general lack of education in the population. These errors diminish as economic development proceeds and the level of education rises; and especially as the people need frequent reference to date of birth or age in their day-to-day activity. Traditionally in Great Britain these errors have been of two types: (i) local preference for certain digital endings, e.g. 0, 2, 8; (ii) biased statements of age, especially the understatement of age by women approaching the middle years of life. The first type are revealed by irregularities in the progression of the figures from age to age, and the extent of such irregularities, as measured by comparison with 'graduated' figures (i.e. figures which have been rendered smooth in progression by mathematical processes), indicate the nature and size of such errors. The second type may be revealed by comparing the census figures at age x with the estimated survivors of those aged x–10 at the previous decennial census after allowing for mortality and migration. The migration element is larger at the younger adult ages; at older ages misstatements of age at death introduce errors in the estimated survivors. As to the first kind of error, the greatest local 'heaping up' has always been at the digital ending 0 where in 1911 the enumerated population was (over ages 23 to 72) 11·7 per cent above the graduated figures. In 1921 this was reduced to 6·3 per cent and in 1931 to 4·4 per cent. In 1966 the excess was only 1·6 per cent. With regard to the second type of error these were regarded as long ago as 1931 as being smaller than could be accounted for by errors in estimating the age structure of migrants in the intercensal periods.

In the census of Great Britain of 1961 the householder was required to record for each member of the household, their sex and 'age in years at *last* birthday and completed months since then'. The question was put in this form as a result of a special investigation carried out after the 1951 Census for which the records of all persons recorded in a sample of census schedules were matched against the corresponding entries in the birth register at the General Register Office. A total of 7,999 persons were matched. The results are shown in detail (together with a full account of the sampling and identification procedures) in the General Report of the 1951

Census (General Register Office, 1958). Despite large sampling errors involved in such a small sample it was possible to claim that the recording of ages at the census was subject to a relatively high order of accuracy. The main factors being a minor degree of digital preference (much less than in earlier censuses), a tendency to anticipate the next birthday (more marked in men than in women) and a small degree of random error. The average net error for males of all ages was $+ \cdot 019$ years (s.e $\cdot 009$) and for females of all ages $- \cdot 001$ (s.e $\cdot 009$).

It was thought that in 1961 the emphasis placed upon *last* birthday together with a request for the completed months would help to correct the tendency to anticipate birthdays. A similar matching of birth and census records (as in 1951) was carried out after the 1961 Census (General Register Office 1968). The majority of errors under a year were of overstatement by about a month and it was suggested that such errors were 'consistent with the age being calculated by subtracting the year and month of birth from April 1961. This simple sum could produce overstatement of a month for people born between the 24th of the month (census date) and the end of the month'. The errors were not large enough to have a significant impact on the quinary age-groups in which most census data are used.

In 1966, presumably in a further effort to avoid either anticipation of birth or the kind of subtraction error noted in 1961, the householder was asked to state the 'sex and date of birth of each person', giving day, month and year. No report is yet available of the effect of this change upon the accuracy of age reporting. It is probable however that in Great Britain a stage has been reached in the reliability of age statements at which any further improvement can only be marginal, the residual error being too small to cause any difficulty in the use of age distributed data, and certainly smaller than the degree of error inherent in other census statements.

It is unnecessary to demonstrate the utility of these topics of age and sex since the related differentials in almost all social and economic factors is self-evident. Age and sex are absolutely basic axes of classification.

9.9 MARITAL CONDITION

The usual form of the census question in Great Britain on this topic is: 'Write "single", "married", "widowed" or "divorced" as appropriate. If separated and not divorced, write "married".' After the census of 1961 a comparison was made between the census figures and the mid-1961 annual population estimate according to marital condition. A considerable part of the differences clearly arose from inadequate information as to the marital condition of immigrants and emigrants between 1951 and 1961 but there were also differences indicative of error in the census statements of marital condition. There was a larger proportion of divorced persons in the population estimate than in the enumerated census population. The difference amounted to about 30 per cent for men aged 27 to 31, decreased with age to the 50–54 age-group and then increased to reach 40 or 50 per cent for those aged 70–74. The proportional errors were less for women, being about 15 per cent at ages 30–34 and 5 per cent at age 40, then increasing with age to about 30 per cent for those aged 70–74. It was concluded that there was a tendency to conceal divorce. There was also in the census figures an excess of women aged 25–39 described as widowed compared with expectation. For women of 30–34 the number of widows enumerated was more than double the number estimated. It was concluded that there was a tendency for single and divorced women enumerated with (illegitimate) children to describe themselves as widowed.

Most of the errors in this particular topic area are deliberate and are therefore difficult to detect by either manual or computer editing. Their incidence is likely to decline as society becomes more permissive.

Marital condition is an important differential in many aspects of census statistics especially housing, household composition and employment and more particularly and obviously, fertility; it is another basic axis of classification.

9.10 FERTILITY

Interest in fertility as the most important element in population growth is general. In countries where fertility is high there is a need to assess the rate of population growth which will both permit, by providing the necessary manpower, and require, by increasing consumer demand, the expansion of industrial productivity. There is a need to attempt to adjust the pace of one to the pace of the other. Where fertility is low there is equally a need to measure it in order to consider whether a restraint upon the expansion of the economy is being influenced and, if inducements to greater fertility are provided (e.g. by family allowances) as part of national policy, to discover whether these inducements appear to be successful.

The complexity of the census fertility analysis ranges from the very crude indication given by the ratio of the number of children in the population to the number of women of fertile age, to detailed distributions of family size by marriage age, and marriage duration.

In order to assess the pace and direction of changes in family building it is necessary to possess serial sets of fertility rates by age at marriage, calendar year of marriage and duration of marriage and, if possible, by birth order. From this information one may see in respect of succeeding marriage cohorts the ultimate size of family likely to be produced and the way in which their fertility is spread over the duration of married life. It is also possible to observe secular changes in the likelihood that a woman who has had, say, two children, will have a third child (Henry, 1953). Finally, the age-duration fertility rates, if stable or moving in a predictable manner, may be used in connection with a nuptiality table to calculate generation replacement rates (General Register Office, 1959). The fertility rates are derived from birth registrations and are not themselves census analyses. The role of the census analysis is to provide (a) controls on the intercensal estimation of populations at risk (b) controls on the year-to-year estimation of family sizes of which the specific fertility rates form increments.

Some rates may be more accurately derived from the census itself. In respect of age, marriage duration, and parity, there is no reason to suppose that at the census the mothers will be differently classified from the way in which, in relation to their offspring, they are classified at birth registration. With regard to socio-economic characteristics (occupations, branch of economic activity, etc.) it is not so; for it is well known that, for example, occupational description may vary significantly not only as between one informant and another but also for the same informant at two different times. This is because a slight change of wording may seriously affect the classification of the occupation. Furthermore, occupation coding is complex and laborious, and if it could be done in respect of the mother and births at the same time the work is much reduced. For this reason an additional question was asked at the 1951 Census of England and Wales; married women were asked to indicate whether they had borne a child in the preceding year. In this way fertility rates, specific for occupation, etc., were derived from the census, for which the populations at risk (the denominators of the rates) were automatically provided by a single process of classification; the occupation, socio-economic group, etc., and the fact of bearing a child within the year of observation (or not doing so) being punched on the same machine card. In consequence it was possible to carry out an investigation of a number of fertility differentials of a social and economic character (General Register Office, 1959) which could not otherwise be studied except with considerably greater strain on data-processing and statistical resources. This device was repeated in the census of 1961 in Great Britain. There was no question directed to fertility in the sample census of 1966.

9.11 DATE OF MARRIAGE

It will be clear from the above that duration of present marriage (and the order of the marriage, i.e. whether first or remarriage) is an important element in the measurement of fertility. In the census of Great Britain of 1961 the question asked of each householder was as follows:

G All married women:
   Write at (i) the date of the present marriage.
   Has she been married more than once?
   Write 'yes' or 'no' at (ii). If 'yes' fill in Column H.
H Widowed or divorced women; OR women married more than once:
   Write at (i) the date of first or only marriage.
   Write at (ii) the date when that marriage ended.

An added note in respect of Col. H stated 'Write at (ii) the date of her first or only husband's death or date of divorce'.

This question makes it possible to distinguish first marriages from other marriages and to calculate either the duration of the current marriage as at census date or the duration of first marriage at which that marriage was broken by widowhood or divorce. All this is necessary in order to calculate a marriage-duration–specific nuptiality table, i.e. a table indicating for a generation of females, traced through life, their entry into and out of the married state and showing for the standing married population at any attained age its distribution by duration of marriage. This is an essential prerequisite for the calculation of generation replacement rates. It is also important to have, at each age of married women, the distribution by marriage duration that would occur in a stable population subject to current mortality and nuptiality experience. This is not likely to be reproduced in the actual population which is never stable but it is a useful control on intercensal population estimates by marriage duration and upon the census enumeration itself, if merely in terms of broad consistency.

In the course of matching work, after the 1961 Census, carried out primarily to check the statements of age at the census and the post-enumeration survey, the opportunity was taken to check the date of marriage for women who were, or had been, married at the time of the census and hence to compare the duration of marriage according to both the census and the post-enumeration survey with that derived from the marriage records. It was, of course, only possible to make this check for women whose marriage could be found in the marriage registration records. Apart from those untraced, all marriages contracted outside England and Wales were excluded. More than 5000 marriages were matched; 89 per cent gave exact agreement as between the census and marriage records and 95 per cent agreed within a year of marriage duration. Those which differed by one year amounted to 2 per cent and there were small numbers showing larger discrepancies. There was no significant bias towards under- or over-statement of marriage duration. In general date of marriage may be regarded as being recorded at the census with a high level of accuracy.

9.12 NUMBER OF CHILDREN BORN

Having considered the denominator of the fertility rate we now turn to the numerator, i.e. the number of births; again this must be specific for marriage duration and age of mother.

In Great Britain the terms of the Census Act 1920 restrict any question about births to those occurring *in* marriage and the census question (addressed to the householder) in 1961 was therefore of the following form:

All married, widowed or divorced women:
Write at (i) the total number of children born alive to her in marriage.
Were any of these children born after 23 April 1960? Write 'yes' or 'no' at (ii).

A note in the instruction stated 'include in the number of children born alive to the mother in marriage, any children of a previous marriage and any that have died'.

The reason for the second part of this question (which yields the numerator for an annual rate) has already been referred to.

In the post-enumeration sample survey, the first part of the question was repeated in two stages, separating the children of the current marriage from those of any previous marriage. This was thought likely to lead to greater accuracy. Some 6000 women were covered in the survey and exact agreement with the original census schedule as to the total number of live-born children was achieved in 96 per cent of them. There was some evidence of overstatement of childlessness due to a failure in 1961 to give specific guidance as to how childless women should answer.

The corresponding question in the 1951 census included an instruction that childless women should state 'none'; in 1961 the absence of such an instruction made it difficult to interpret those cases in which the space was left blank or filled by a stroke. Out of 396 such cases successfully checked in the post-enumeration survey, 81 per cent were childless; in the main census processing all such cases were treated as childless. The net overstatement of childlessness in first marriages was estimated at about 6·5 per cent. Apart from this error, there was no evidence of significant errors in the number of live-born children.

9.13 INTERNAL MIGRATION

The urbanization which accompanies industrialization in all countries results, in many, in large internal migratory movements of population. In turn this migration may have extensive demographic effects in changing population structure in different parts of the country and in producing mortality and fertility differentials. Even where economic development is already advanced, there are continuous changes in the geographical distribution of industry especially as old industries decline and new industries develop and this leads to streams of movement the direction and pace of which must be studied in the interest of effective urban planning. Internal migration has become, again as part of the economic orientation in population studies, an important topic of demographic analysis. In many countries questions of the type, 'Were you living at this address a year ago? If so, how long have you lived here? If not, what was the address of your usual residence a year ago?' have been introduced into the population census.

Movements may be classified by the type – for example, rural to rural, rural to urban, urban to rural; within the same region and outside the region of former residence. These movement types may then be cross-tabulated with sex, age, occupation, branch of economic activity, socio-economic group, and household and family structure. There can also be a cross-tabulation of area of present residence and area of former residence, so as to show up the main streams of movement taking place within the country. Further, the movers themselves may be treated as a selected population and a special study can be made of their social and economic characteristics.

In the census of Great Britain of 1966 the following questions were asked:

5. If the person's *usual address one year ago* (on 24 April 1965) was the same as that given in reply to question 4[1] write 'same'. If not, write the usual address on 24 April 1965. For children under one year old, write 'under one'.
6. If the person's usual address five years ago (on 24 April 1961) was the same as that given in reply to question 5 write 'same'. If not write the usual address on 24 April 1961. For children under five years old write 'under five'.

At the time of writing there is no published evaluation of the response to question 6. It seems likely to have caused difficulty since it refers to question 5 not question 4 (as does question 5) and this may not always have been noticed. It therefore identifies moves between 24 April 1961 and 24 April 1965, i.e. the first four years of the five-year period ending on census day. It presents a severe challenge to memory. Given the high level of mobility of the British population it is difficult to see the additional value of this four-year rate of movement, covering, as it did, the abnormal period immediately prior to the Commonwealth Immigration Act. Question 5 (which was also asked at the 1961 Census and answered reliably) would seem to provide an entirely adequate basis for the calculation of current annual rates of movement. In the introductory notes to the published tables for 1966 the General Register Office state that 'sample checks are being made on the question asking for the address five years before the census. The information given on the 1966 schedules is being compared with that given at the 1961 Census and there are indications that there may be appreciable errors in the answers to this question'.

Both questions 5 and 6 are related to 'usual residence'. The post-enumeration survey after the 1961 Census indicated that

---

[1] The question on usual residence.

a fraction of the order of 10 per cent had a claim to more than one usual address. A large proportion of these are school-children and students or members of the Armed Forces. Clear instructions were given in the notes to the census schedule that schoolchildren should give their home address and the Armed Forces their married quarter or home address. It appears that this instruction was followed in respect of most school children and for a large proportion of the Forces personnel.

No instructions were given on the census schedule or the notes to other classes of persons with more than one residence and they were free to choose whatever residence they pleased. The post-enumeration survey revealed no clear pattern of behaviour even where they normally spent the week and the week-end at the address of enumeration. It was suggested that clearer instructions would be needed in future censuses to clarify the position of those with more than one usual residence.

The post-enumeration survey also showed that of those recorded as usually resident in the household but temporarily absent on census night (Part III of the 10 per cent sample), 79 per cent of this group, counting schoolchildren and Forces, were clearly residents of the household. The remaining 21 per cent all had more than one residence and 56 per cent of these were not normally resident during the week. This indicated the possibility of duplication between people returned as absent members of one household and those returned as residents of another household.

The 1961 post-enumeration survey indicated that, on the whole, the migration question was reliably answered. A small proportion of alleged migrants (those who had changed their usual residence in the previous year) failed to give a previous address and in the non-migrants (who, in 1961, were asked how long they had lived at their census address) there were a small number of errors in the duration statement; these errors were of the expected type, e.g. total omission or rounding up.

9.14 IMMIGRATION FROM OUTSIDE THE COUNTRY

It may be necessary to examine international migration separately from internal migration. For various reasons, sometimes ethnic origin and cultural association, more often social and economic, immigrants from outside the country may present special problems in employment, housing, and education, and in other aspects of social administration.

While the 'movement question' referred to above identifies those who have moved within a specified interval of time and with further reference to previous address permits the separation of the main stream of movement from outside the national boundaries, it provides no indication of the size, internal distribution, or national affinity of the total immigrant population which may have accumulated over several decades. Two further questions, on birthplace and nationality, may help to elucidate this aspect of population structure.

9.15 BIRTHPLACE

The question asked at the 1966 Census in Great Britain was:

> If born in England, Wales, Scotland or Ireland write the name of the town or village and the county of the mother's usual address at the time of the person's birth. If this address was in London write the name of the district. If born overseas write the name of the country of birth.

The notes to the questions contained an instruction that 'if the mother's usual residence at the time of a person's birth is known, give the name and address of the hospital, nursing home or actual place of birth. If born at sea write "at sea".'

The answers to the first part of the question provide the same indication of cumulative movement within Great Britain and Ireland as the second part does for immigrants from overseas. It is of doubtful value since the British population has become highly urbanized and highly mobile and the 'end state' at any one census gives no clue as to the routes by which the population has reached that state. In 1961 the question related only to country of birth.

For immigrants from overseas, at least for the older members of this group who were born in their country of origin, identification of country of birth does permit a broad classification of regions of the world from which they have come.

9.16 NATIONALITY

There was no question on nationality in 1966 but in the 1961 Census of Great Britain, the following question was addressed to householders in respect of persons *not* born in Great Britain or Northern Ireland:

(a) If a citizen of the Commonwealth state at (i) citizenship, e.g. United Kingdom and Colonies, Indian, Canadian.

(b) If a citizen of the United Kingdom and Colonies, state at (ii) whether citizen by birth, descent, naturalization, registration, marriage, etc.

(c) For other persons state at (i) nationality, e.g. Italian, Polish, Yugoslav.

A significant proportion of people failed to state their nationality. The post-enumeration survey indicated that a large proportion of these were in fact 'United Kingdom and Colonies'. A tenth of those who were citizens of the United Kingdom and Colonies used the expression 'British' which is still colloquially popular though it has no legal status or meaning.

9.17 LANGUAGE

It has been suggested that a further pointer to the country of origin might be a question on language, e.g. mother tongue or language normally spoken in the house. The response to such a question tends however to be unspecific owing to the universality of some languages (for example English) and the true situation so far as language of original country is concerned is often overlaid by the exigencies of higher education, marriage or employment and sometimes distorted for political reasons (a strongly nationalistic person may pretend to a language medium which he never in fact uses). In some parts of the world however language is an important determinant of the local needs for educational services. The important distinction between *ability* to speak a language and customary *use* of language has to be borne in mind. It has been a traditional practice in Great Britain to ask in Wales a question about ability to speak Welsh; and, in Scotland, about ability to speak Gaelic. The answers are not, of course, a measure of the habitual use of those languages. Those who claim to speak *only* Welsh, *are* a specific group. Those who claim to speak both Welsh and English range from those who regularly speak Welsh to those who learned Welsh in childhood but who speak the language on rare occasions and not fluently.

Quite apart from the use of language as an indication of country of origin, the possible concentration of groups of non-English-speaking people (for example, Urdu-speaking Pakistani in Bradford) is of considerable importance to local government since for effective contact local officials have to be found who are proficient in the relevant languages. This problem extends to the holding of the census itself; it will in such circumstances be necessary to print a supply of census forms in these languages otherwise response will be jeopardized.

9.18 URBAN AND RURAL POPULATION

Returning for a moment to the study of urbanization, it is important to be able to separate the population into urban and rural elements and to examine the size and disposition of recognizable concentrations or clusters of population.

This involves establishing conventions for the identification of population clusters. The most practical method is to work with large-scale maps which reveal street formation and the disposition of scattered buildings. The population of such street formations or scattered buildings which are not separated by more than a specified distance may be regarded as comprising one cluster. For this purpose administrative boundaries are ignored,[1] as the concept of the cluster is quite distinct from that of the local authority area. The clusters and any residual scattered buildings are then grouped into localities, i.e. population groups forming a unity indicated by social and economic interdependence in their daily lives. Localities may then be classified as urban or rural on the basis of population size and the distribution of the active population by industry. The criterion of size of population can be used to distinguish three categories consisting of small, medium-sized, and large localities. Some countries use 2000 as the dividing line between the first two categories and 10,000 as the dividing line between the second and third.

A second criterion of industrial activity can be used to distinguish within the smallest size group between agricultural and non-agricultural localities. These localities in which the proportion of the active population engaged in agriculture exceeds say 20 per cent would be classed as rural agricultural localities and the others as rural non-agricultural localities.

This would mean that four basic categories would be distinguished, namely, rural agricultural, rural non-agricultural, intermediate, and urban localities.

The next stage in classification would be to break down the heterogeneous intermediate category, either by the application

---

[1] It should be borne in mind that we are dealing here with a special purpose, and not a complete alternative to administrative areas which must still form the basis of the main census tabulations.

of the simple criterion of the proportion of the active population engaged in agriculture, or by the separation of the proportions engaged in agriculture, industry, and service activities or, if the necessary data be available, by reference to such criteria as the presence of an administrative centre, the type of building (one-storey or multi-storey), availability of hospitals, etc. Localities can also be classified according to their functional type (industrial centre, university centre, holiday resort, etc.). The general question of urban typology is discussed later.

9.19 OCCUPATION AND BRANCH OF ECONOMIC ACTIVITY

Tabulations indicating the distribution of skills in the labour force and the apportionment of the labour force among the different branches of economic activity are of fundamental importance to labour recruitment and mobility, to measurement of the development of branches of economic activity, and to an appreciation of the economic characteristics of population groups. The general interest in the provision of comparable statistics for international comparative studies of economic development is evident from the establishment of international standard classifications of other occupations (I.S.C.O.) and branch of economic activity (I.S.I.C.). There are also international recommendations on the subsidiary classification of the active population by employment status, viz.:

Employers.
Workers on own account.
Employees.
Family workers.
Members of producer's co-operatives.

In the past developments in analyses have been less in the

direction of elaborating the basic distributions of occupation and industrial groups by sex, age, and employment status, than in cross-tabulation with other characteristics such as housing, education, or fertility, or household structure. There is nevertheless a growing recognition of the need for further subdivision of skill and function within the framework of minimal standard classifications. Most broad occupational groupings are concerned with separating managers, non-manual workers, skilled, semi-skilled, and unskilled workmen. Not only are the assignments to these groups somewhat arbitrary but the groups themselves are large, unwieldy, and heterogeneous. It seems likely that either by utilizing non-census data on types of training required (especially distinguishing re-employment from in-service training) or by cross-tabulation with census data on education, duration of employment, and employment status, it might be possible to break up these groups into an approximation to levels of skills, or responsibility.

There is considerable interest in the separation of the managerial element in industry; in the distinction between the makers of policy and those who, albeit with some elbow-room of discretion, merely carry out a prescribed policy. The relationship of the managerial to the non-managerial labour force in different industries throws light upon the development of the organizational structure. Here again a single group of managers is too large and heterogeneous, and splits are made according to branch of economic activity (agriculture, extractive industry, productive industry, distribution, government, etc.) and also by size of establishment (total number of workers). With regard to this latter factor of size it would, of course, be more meaningful to classify managers by the number of workers they manage, but this would require a specific question, and it would be naïve to expect reliable answers. If 'manager' is incorporated into the employment status classification as well as in the classification of occupations, then a single tabulation of the economically active by branch of economic activity and status is sufficient for all these purposes. Such a tabulation shows, for example, from one census to another, the trend in the proportion of 'own account' workers (a downward trend indicating the organization of industry in larger units) and in the incidence of the 'family worker' status as a general indicator of economic development.

In order to provide information relating to the inter-industry or inter-occupation (as distinct from geographical) mobility of labour, as a background to the assessment of economic stability or flexibility, tabulations may usefully be made of 'duration of present employment' (in relation to age). Such a distribution shows to what extent labour is mobile and to what extent the occupation and industries recorded may be regarded as 'usual'. Another kind of tabulation which is partly related to labour mobility is that of secondary occupations. This is only relevant to countries where there are significant numbers of workers with more than one occupation, either simultaneously or consecutively within a short time interval; to every secondary occupation there would also be a secondary industry and a secondary employment status. To be useful the tabulation must be presented as a cross-tabulation of primary and secondary occupations (and industries), and this is a formidable undertaking.

Another aspect of labour statistics, in respect of which in some countries there is a tendency to regard the population census as the source, is that of hours of employment per week. A tabulation showing a distribution of hours of work for each occupation and industry provides an indication of relative working conditions in different avenues of employment; furnishes information on under-employment where it exists; and serves to provide standards for regulating social security schemes. For this latter purpose it is useful also to have tabulation of frequency and method of payment.

9.20 SOCIO-ECONOMIC GROUPING

One of the most interesting of modern developments in demographic analyses, and one which illustrates forcefully the increased emphasis upon economic aspects of population statistics, has been the production of socio-economic groupings. In order to observe the interrelationship of population trends (in the wider sense which embraces cultural and behavioural changes) and economic factors, it is necessary to divide the population into groups which are homogeneous in respect of the level of living (in material terms), educational background, and community of interest in the widest sense.

Two alternative approaches have been made. The first method is to attribute to each of the occupations distinguished in the classification a ranking based either on social values, for example, that of standing within the community (such as in the United Kingdom from the 1911 census onward),[1] or on a score derived from a battery of such values. This has two disadvantages:

(i) There is a likelihood that the ranking will be influenced by preconceived notions of just those differentials of health or behaviour which the groupings are to be used to discover.

(ii) It is difficult to provide an economic interpretation of the ultimate interrelationship of the groups and other social characteristics because of the abstract and subjective character of the ranking.

A second method has therefore been developed which is of a

---

[1] Under this system, which is still in use, especially for occupational mortality purposes, every occupation (and therefore every person who follows it) is assigned to one of five social classes (really occupational classes), viz. (I) Professional, etc., (II) Intermediate, (III) Skilled workers, (IV) Partly skilled workers, (V) Unskilled workers.

much more objective character in that it is derived automatically from a cross-tabulation of the four economic classifications already referred to, viz.:

(i) Type of activity in the economy
(ii) Occupation
(iii) Employment status
(iv) Branch of economic activity (industry)

The individual cells of such a cross-tabulation represent groups with substantial homogeneity of social and economic characteristics, and these can be gathered into broader groups to the extent of contraction in numbers of groups that may be desired. An important feature of these groups is the fact that they are not necessarily ranked in any preconceived order; it is claimed only that they are economically different, not that one group has higher social standing than another. Clearly in material terms the level of living is higher for one group than another, so that some degree of economic ordering is inevitable.

The European Working Group on Population Census of E.C.E., has subjected this system to close study and has recommended the following combinations:

Socio-Economic Classification

A. Economically active population:

1. Farm-employers.
2. Farmers on own account without employees.
3. Members of agricultural producers' co-operatives.
4. Agricultural workers.
5. Employers in industry and commerce; large enterprises.
6. Employers in industry and commerce; small enterprises.
7. Employers in industry and commerce; own account workers without employees.
8. Liberal and related professions.

9. Members of non-agricultural producers' co-operatives.
10. Directors (managers) of enterprises and companies.
11. Senior non-manual workers.
12. Intermediate and junior non-manual workers and sales workers.
13. Supervisors and skilled, semi-skilled and specialized manual workers.
14. Labourers.
15. Service staff (domestic servants, cleaners, caretakers) and related workers.
16. Members of armed forces on compulsory military service.
17. Economically active persons not classifiable in the above groups.

B. Economically inactive population:

18. Former farm-employers.
19. Former non-agricultural employers.
20. Former employees.
21. Other independent inactive persons.

      ———————

22. Children below minimum school-leaving age.
23. Students and schoolchildren above minimum school-leaving age.
24. Housewives.
25. Other adults in the home.
26. Inmates of institutions.

(Further subdivisions were suggested, and also summary groups, but these have been omitted in the interests of brevity.)

These socio-economic groups may then be used to classify the whole population (attributing to dependants the groups of those on whom they are dependent) or the active population only, or whole households (by the group of the chief economic supporter).

As in the case of the analysis of household structure, this socio-economic grouping is essentially a matter of exploiting information already provided on the census schedule; it does not involve additional specific questions. In the 1961 Census and subsequently in Great Britain a broad classification in sixteen socio-economic groups based on these principles has been adopted. They are defined in the introduction to the published census occupational classification but in brief they are:

1. Employers and managers in central and local government, industry, commerce, etc. – large establishments.
   Persons who employ others or generally plan and supervise in non-agricultural enterprises employing twenty-five or more persons.

2. Employers and managers in industry, commerce, etc. – small establishments.
   As in 1. but in establishments employing fewer than twenty-five persons.

3. Professional workers – self-employed.
   Self-employed persons engaged in work normally requiring qualifications of university degree standard.

4. Professional workers – employees.
   Employees engaged in work normally requiring qualifications of university degree standard.

5. Intermediate non-manual workers.
   Employees, not exercising general planning or supervisory powers, engaged in non-manual occupations ancillary to the professions but not normally requiring qualifications of university degree standard; persons engaged in artistic work and not employing others threat; and persons engaged in occupations otherwise included in Group 5 who have an additional and formal supervisory function.

6. Junior non-manual workers.
   Employees, not exercising general planning or supervisory powers, engaged in clerical, sales and non-manual

communications and security occupations, excluding those who have additional and formal supervisory functions.

7. Personal service workers.

Employees engaged in service occupations caring for food, drink, clothing and other personal needs.

8. Foremen and supervisors – manual.

Employees (other than managers) who formally and immediately supervise others engaged in manual occupations, whether or not themselves engaged in such occupations.

9. Skilled manual workers.

Employees engaged in manual occupations which require considerable and specific skills.

10. Semi-skilled manual workers.

Employees engaged in manual occupations which require slight but specific skills.

11. Unskilled manual workers.

Other employees engaged in manual occupations.

12. Own account workers (other than professional).

Self-employed persons engaged in any trade, personal service or manual occupation not normally requiring training of university degree standard and having no employees other than family workers.

13. Farmers – employers and managers.

Persons who own, rent or manage farms, market gardens or forests, employing people other than family workers in the work of the enterprise.

14. Farmers – own account.

Persons who own or rent farms, market gardens or forests and having no employees other than family workers.

15. Agricultural workers.

Employees engaged in tending crops, animals, game or forests or operating agricultural or forestry machinery.

16. Members of armed forces.

9.21 SECTOR OF THE ECONOMY

As has already been demonstrated, the economic information provided on the census schedule may be organized in a number of different ways. One additional way is to divide the active population between the public and private sectors of the economy by reference to branch of economic activity, occupation, and employment status. This is particularly of interest in countries where it is desired to observe the extent and pace of socialization of industry. Such an analysis is also of importance in any planned economy where it is desired, for example, to maintain a balanced programme of expansion as between the different sectors and it is necessary to observe the related manpower problems.

9.22 WORKPLACE

Where many people live in one locality and work in another, as in the United Kingdom, the geographical distribution of numbers of workers in different branches of economic activity has to be carried out on the basis of the area in which the workplace is situated as distinct from the area of residence of the worker. Since, in these circumstances, the address of residence and the address of the workplace are both recorded on the one schedule it is possible to attach area codes to these addresses and to carry out two types of analysis:

(i) Measurement of the difference between the day and night populations of urban localities and an examination of the character of the net inward movement each day and its distribution by sex, age, occupation, etc.

(ii) A cross-tabulation of area of residence and area of workplace to indicate the lines of journey (since the tabulation has to be in terms of persons crossing specific area boundaries, movements within a specific area are excluded and long and short movements across the boundary are given equal weight. Coding should therefore be to the smallest areal unit permissible).

These analyses are of value to transport authorities who want to know the pattern of movement and the social and economic characteristics of those who journey to work; and to town planning authorities who have to consider whether such movement is tolerable or could be avoided by re-siting industry or residential centres, or both. An increasing volume of movement to work is also of interest as indicating a later stage of town development in which the mixed market, residential, and cultural core is displaced by the growing commercial centre; and when the diminishing residential accommodation and the noise and atmospheric pollution of expanding factory and office areas compel workers to seek dwellings in more open spaces on the periphery of the town.

9.23 CLASSIFICATION OF OCCUPATIONS AND INDUSTRIES (BRANCHES OF ECONOMIC ACTIVITY)

A classification of occupations compiled by the General Register Offices of England and Wales and of Scotland specifically for use in the population census has become widely accepted for statistical purposes. It is normally revised and reissued as an H.M.S.O. publication (*Classification of Occupations*) a year or so before each census. A more detailed, i.e. more job-content-specific, classification is used for placement purposes by the Department of Employment and Productivity but this is not intended for statistical purposes and is not used in census work. Both classifications are related to (i.e. translatable into) the International Statistical Classification of Occupations compiled by the International Labour Office; international comparability is therefore secured.

There are four separate aspects of the employment or former employment of a person:

(1) Economic position (active or inactive).

(2) Employment status (e.g. self-employed, apprentice, etc.).

(3) Industry (commonly referred to as branch of economic activity).

(4) Occupation.

The classification by *economic position* distinguishes first the economically active from the inactive. Among the active we separate family workers (those living in the same household as their employer) from other occupied persons and those out of employment. There is a further division of each of the two occupied groups into full-time and part-time; those out of employment may be split into (*a*) sick (*b*) others. The economically inactive are subdivided into institutional inmates, the retired, students, and others who are inactive. There are a number of important matters of definition which apply especially here and also to the other classifications. First there is a need for a time reference. The question 'are you employed?' naturally evokes the question, 'When – today, yesterday, usually, ever?' It is usual therefore to define a point of time (a particular day) or a short period (for example, the week before the census), to which all the information is related. When is a person *in* employment? It is usual to agree, conventionally, that those absent on account of strikes, lockouts, short-time working, sickness (unless employment has actually terminated for this reason) or holidays are to be regarded as in employment.

A mere statement of occupation is not sufficient either to determine level of living or occupational health risk (if any) or training content or job content unless qualified by a statement indicating whether the occupation in the individual case is followed in a supervisory or operational capacity; whether in an employed or an employer capacity. This qualification is classified under the heading of employment status, as follows:

9.24 EMPLOYMENT STATUS

A. Self-employed
   (1) without employees
   (2) with employees
      (*a*) large establishments
      (*b*) small establishments

B. Employees
   (1) Managers
      (*a*) large establishments
      (*b*) small establishments
   (2) Foremen and supervisors
      (*a*) manual
      (*b*) non-manual
   (3) Apprentices, articled pupils, formal trainees
   (4) Employees (not elsewhere classified)

A self-employed person is one not employed by any person or company and persons working in their own home for an employer (outworkers). Directors of limited companies are excluded from this category. 'Without employees' means without paid assistance other than family workers. A large establishment is one with twenty-five or more persons.

9.25 INDUSTRY

Here we are concerned with the trade carried on by firms, not the *jobs* performed by individuals in the furtherance of that trade.

For all official purposes there is a Standard Industrial Classification which is revised from time to time by a Government interdepartmental committee. The last issue was in 1958. It conforms, generally, to the International Standard Industrial Classification of all Economic Activities issued by the United Nations.

The classification is based on industries without regard to

their nature of ownership or operation. Manufacturing units owned or operated by the Central Government are classified in the same way as those in private hands and are not classified industrially as 'national government service' (government *is* one form of economic activity). Transport services operated by local authorities are likewise included under 'transport' and not under 'local government service'.

The unit of classification is the 'establishment'. This is normally the whole of the premises, such as a farm, a mine, a factory or a shop at a particular address. All activities at that address (including, for example, departments engaged in selling, bottling, packing, transport, etc.) are included. There are exceptions. If at a single address, there are two or more departments engaged in different activities in respect of which separate records are available, each department is treated as a separate establishment.

There are some 150 Minimum List Headings distinguished by arabic numerals (3 digits). These Minimum List Headings have been grouped into 24 Orders distinguished by roman numerals.

In the actual classification some special points arise.

(*a*) Merchanting: establishments mainly engaged in merchanting, broking, importing and exporting are classified as in the distributive trades and not in the industry or trade producing the goods for which they are an outlet.

(*b*) Head Office: the head office of a firm operating in the United Kingdom is classified as far as possible according to the major activity of the firm. Head offices of firms trading abroad and not carrying on a substantial trading activity in the United Kingdom are classified to a heading in Miscellaneous Services.

(*c*) Repair work: where the bulk of the repair work on goods of any particular type is carried out by manufacturers, any establishments specializing in the repair of these goods are classified to manufacturing. Where most of the repairs are carried out at establishments whose main business is distribution, the specialist repair establishments are also classified to distribution. For example, establishments repairing radio and television sets, watches and clocks, furniture, etc., are classified to the distributive trades; those engaged in the repair of ships, locomotives, aircraft, and most kinds of plant and machinery are classified to manufacturing industry.

9.26 OCCUPATION

The 1960 classification contains about 200 unit groups and, subject to the overriding requirements of the British Census and other social or medical studies associated with the census and the preservation of as much comparability as possible with previous classifications, has been based on the International Standard Classification of Occupation, recommended by the International Labour Office[1] for use in National Censuses (it is broadly comparable with the 2 digit level of the International Classification).

The basic common factor of all groups is the kind of work done and the nature of the operation performed. But if, by reason of the material worked in, the degree of skill involved, the physical energy required, the environmental conditions, the social and economic status associated with the occupation, or any combination of these factors, unit groups based solely on kind of work were too comprehensive they have been further broken down on the basis of these other factors in order to identify what are substantially separate occupations.

[1] International Labour Office, International Standard Classification of Occupations, Geneva 1958.

Certain limiting conditions have also operated, e.g. that the number of individuals likely to be included in a unit is sufficiently large to be worth separate identification, that the identification of a unit group is likely to be tolerably complete and accurate from the limited information obtained from a census, that there is sufficient potential interest in the group to justify separate identification, and that statistics for the group could not be obtained from the cross classification of occupation by employment status or industry.

The unit groups obtained by the above process have been grouped into orders: these larger groups, like the unit groups, have certain broad features of occupation in common.

Certain groups of persons in employment, in particular the self-employed and the managers, give rise to difficult conceptual problems.

Self-employed. Even within the same field of economic activity self-employed persons range from the working craftsman to the owner and manager of a large industrial concern, extremes for which a single occupational code is not appropriate. But there is no general rule that can be formulated about the size of the undertaking that requires the owner to be occupied mainly on managerial work and, moreover, especially in mortality and morbidity investigation, the available data affords no indication of the size of undertaking involved. It is assumed that most self-employed persons control or operate only small enterprises, so that they are not allocated to the managerial group but to an appropriate specific skill. Where self-employed persons form an important group whose occupational assignment is not self-evident, a specific mention is made in the occupational unit group concerned. Owners of services, such as typewriting, office cleaning, car hire, with regard to whom there is no evidence that they perform the actual work associated with such services, are classified as persons *selling* services.

The growing recognition of management as an occupation in itself, which is to a certain extent independent of the particular field in which it is exercised, has led to managers being classified in a main order of 'administrators and managers'. There are exceptions because in some fields, mainly services, the title of manager is given to persons with comparatively limited responsibilities, and also because in some cases the main activity is that of an occupation other than management. In the first category would come the shop manager and in the second the ship's captain. These persons are given the employment status code of manager but are not coded to the Management Order of the occupation classification.

Professionally and technically qualified persons are classified as managers if in actual charge, at a level above that of works foreman, of the execution of a task either directly or through subordinate managers unless the task so supervised is a professional or technical service.

Foremen. Foremen (other than road and rail transport operating foremen who are classified as supervisors in transport), are classified with the workers they control and distinguished in the status coding.

Labourers. The groups in the classification assigned to labourers are strictly limited to persons performing occupations requiring little or no training or experience and for this reason certain groups of persons who have some degree of skill but are returned as labourers, e.g. fitter's labourers, are excluded.

Allocation to these groups is on a strictly industrial basis, thus departing from the general basis of classification elsewhere; the industry concerned is that of the 'establishment' taken as a whole.

Apprentices, articled pupils and learners are classified to the group appropriate to those whose training is completed. Graduate and student apprentices are classified to the professional occupation for which they are training.

Armed Forces. For the various economic activity and social classification it is intended to keep distinct all uniformed members of the Services, and medical personnel and chaplains are accordingly assigned to the groups for Armed Forces, and not to their professional unit group.

9.27 THE CENSUS QUESTIONS ON EMPLOYMENT

It will be clear from this discussion of data utilization that the census questions on employment must have specific reference to (*a*) whether in employment or not at a particular time (*b*) the occupation (*c*) full-time or part-time (*d*) status (*e*) industry. The actual set of questions asked at the 1966 Census of Great Britain for persons aged 15 and over, were:

10.	Has the person had any job at any time during the twelve months ended 23 April 1966? (See Notes.) Write 'Yes' or 'No'. If 'Yes' answer question 11. If 'No' go on to question 19. 10
11.	Has the person had any job at any time during the week ended 23 April 1966? (See Notes.) Write 'Yes' or 'No'. If 'Yes' answer questions 12 to 18. If 'No' go on to question 19. 11

> 12. Write the name and business of the person's main employer during the week. (See Notes.) But if mainly self-employed write either 'Self-employed, employs others' or 'Self-employed without employees' and also the name and nature of the business. If a trading name is used write that name.   12

For people with a job in the week ended 23 April	13. (a) What was the person's occupation in the employment given in reply to question 12? Where appropriate state the material worked or dealt in and for workers at mines whether the job was mainly above or below ground. (See Notes.) 13 (a) (b) If appropriate write 'Apprentice', 'Learner' (only if in skilled craft), 'Articled clerk', 'Articled pupil', 'Student apprentice', 'Graduate apprentice' or 'Management trainee'. (See Notes.) (b)

14. (a) Was the job given in reply to question 13 full-time? (See Notes.) Write 'Yes' or 'No'.   14 (a)

(b) If 'No' how many hours, excluding meal breaks, did the person work in that job in the week ended 23 April? (See Notes.)   (b)

15. What was the full address of the place of work for the job given in reply to question 13? (For transport workers, building workers, dock workers, seamen and people with no regular place of work, see Notes.) If the work is carried on mainly at home write 'At home'.   15

16. What method of transport does the person normally use for the longest part, by distance, of the journey to the place of work given in reply to question 15? (See Notes.) If the person walks all or most of the way to work write 'On foot'.   16

| | 17. | (a) | Did the person do any other work for payment or profit during the week ended 23 April 1966 in addition to the work described in reply to questions 12 and 13? (See Notes.) Write 'Yes' or 'No' | 17(a) |

For people with a job in week ended 23 April

17. (a) Did the person do any other work for payment or profit during the week ended 23 April 1966 in addition to the work described in reply to questions 12 and 13? (See Notes.) Write 'Yes' or 'No' 17(a)

(b) If 'Yes' was any of this additional work as an employee? Write 'Yes' or 'No'. (b)

18. Did the person have a job on Monday, 18 April 1966? (See Notes.) Write 'Yes' or 'No'. If 'Yes' go on to question 22. If 'No' answer questions 19 to 21. 18

For people who did not have a job on Monday 18 April

19. On Monday, 18 April 1966, was the person:

(a) Registered at a Ministry of Labour Employment Exchange or Youth Employment Office? Write 'Yes' or 'No'. 19(a)

(b) Seeking work but not registered at a Ministry of Labour Employment Exchange or Youth Employment Office? Write 'Yes' or 'No'. (b)

(c) Unable to seek work because of temporary sickness or injury? Write 'Yes' or 'No'. (c)

(d) Waiting to take up a job starting on 24 April or later? Write 'Yes' or 'No'. (d)

(e) Wholly retired? Write 'Yes' or 'No'. (e)

(f) Not seeking work for any other reason? Please specify. For example, write 'Housewife', 'Home duties', 'Permanent sickness', 'Disablement', 'Studying', 'Private means'. (f)

For
people
who
did
not
have a
job on
Monday,
18 April

> 20. Write the name and business of the person's last full-time employer, but if formerly self-employed write either 'Self-employed, employed others' or 'Self-employed without employees' and also the name and nature of the business. (See Notes.)
>
> For students, housewives or persons who are occupied solely on home duties no answer need be given to this question or to question 21.   20
>
> ---
>
> 21. What was the person's occupation in the employment given in reply to question 20? Where appropriate state the material worked or dealt in and for workers at mines whether the job was mainly above or below ground. (See Notes.)   21

Question 10

This question was designed to separate those who had not yet entered employment or who had been out of employment for one year or more. A 'job' was defined as 'any work for payment or profit including service in H.M. Forces' and as including, in particular, '(i) work on a person's own account (ii) part-time work, even if only for a few hours, such as jobbing gardening or paid domestic work (iii) casual or temporary work of any kind (for example, seasonal work, week-end work and vacation work by students) (iv) unpaid work in a family business including a shop or farm'. Unpaid work except in a family business (where some profit was assumed to accrue) did not count as a job.

Question 11

This established whether or not the person was in employment at the time reference defined as the week prior to census day; all subsequent questions relate to this interval of time. Notes to the schedule made it clear that, as well as people who attended work for pay or profit in the week before the census, the following people also counted as having a job during that week:

(1) People away from work on holiday if their job was waiting for them on their return.
(2) People away from work because of illness or injury if their job was waiting for them on their return.
(3) People away from work because of a strike or other industrial dispute.
(4) People laid off work by the employers for that week.

Question 12

This question is directed to determining the industry in which the person is employed. It is not possible to expect an employed person to describe the industry of his employer with sufficient specificity to permit adequate classification. In most cases he will know too little about the main industry and it is most unlikely that he will know the classification requirements. The procedure in Great Britain is therefore to seek the assistance of the Department of Employment and Productivity in the construction of a list of all establishments in which there are at least twenty-five employees and which on the basis of knowledge in the possession of the D.E.P. are already assigned to rubrics of the industrial classification. Given the name and address of the employer a coding clerk has merely to identify the establishment in the list and can then copy the industry code number on to the schedule. The census question therefore asks for the name and address of the employer. It also asks for the nature of the business to be stated (*a*) as a check on identification (*b*) to enable small establishments (not on the General Register Office list) to be classified.

The notes to question 12 state:

(i) Describe the nature of the employer's business fully, avoiding abbreviations or initials. General terms such as 'Manufacturers', 'Merchants', 'Agents', 'Brokers', 'Dealers', 'Engineering' are not enough by themselves and further details should be given about the articles manufactured or dealt in.

(ii) 'Self-employed, employs others' means having one or more employees who are not family workers. (A family worker is one who lives in the same household as the employer and is related to him.)

(iii) For civil servants, local government officers and other public officials give the name of the Government Department or Local Authority and the branch in which they are employed.

(iv) For people employed solely in private domestic service there is no need to give the names of individual employers during the week; it is enough to write 'Private' in answer to this question.

(v) For people who changed their job during the week give details of the job held at the end of the week.

Question 13

This question is designed to get a description of the job sufficient to enable it to be coded according to the Classification of Occupations referred to above. This is why reference is made in the question to 'the material worked or dealt in' and special reference is made to mining and, in this connexion, to whether or not it is surface work. (On previous occasions a comparison of census records and National Coal Board staff records had shown that there is a tendency for a coal miner to retain this job description even when for health or other reasons he has been transferred from the coal face to lighter work on the surface.) It will be noted that the question is as self-contained as possible; nevertheless certain supplementary notes are essential as follows:

(i) Full and precise details of occupation are required. If a person's job is known in the trade or industry by a special name, use that name. Terms such as 'Scientist', 'Technician', 'Engineer', 'Machinist', 'Fitter', 'Foreman', 'Checker', should not be used by themselves. Greater detail should be given as, for example, 'Wood-working Machinist', 'Civil Engineer', 'Tool room Foreman', etc.

(ii) For civil servants, local government officers and other public officials, give their rank or grade.

The second part of the question, 13(*b*) is necessary to identify those who are still in training and who, therefore, cannot be regarded as fully productive in their intended occupation. It also provides a measure of the extent to which the occupation is skilled and requires preliminary training; and therefore of the extent to which manpower planning must take account of the period during which individuals are absorbed in the 'pipe-line' of training and of the resources which must be diverted to such training. A note to the question stated:

This part of the question should be answered for anyone undergoing training for a period fixed in advance and leading to recognition as a skilled worker or technician and/or a recognized technical, commercial or professional qualification or managerial post. It should not be answered for a young person undergoing probationary training who has not yet entered into formal apprenticeship.

Question 14

For manpower purposes it is clearly important to know how many of the units are full-time and if part-time what equivalent full-time units are represented. For this reason it is necessary to ask part-time workers how many hours a week they were working at the time of the census, i.e. in the reference week. The following notes were added:

14 (*a*) Write 'Yes' if employment is normally full-time but was interrupted during the week (for example by sickness, injury, holidays, short-time workings, strikes or unfavourable weather) or was started or stopped part way through the week.

(*b*) For part-time workers not at work during that particular week write 'None'.

Question 15

The place of work may not be the same as the address of the employer given in answer to question 12. It is necessary to ask for the precise place of work partly to indicate whether the establishment referred to in question 12 is the centre of an organization which has branches (this may affect the industrial coding if the branch is devoted to a specialized activity in a diversified trading complex) and partly to enable the destination of the journey to work to be fixed. For certain kinds of mobile workers there is no regular place of work and rules have to be laid down to deal with these. The instructions on the schedule state:

(i) For people with no regular place of work such as sales representatives, transport inspectors, certain building workers and others who do not work daily at or from a fixed address or depot, write 'No fixed place'.

(ii) For people working daily at or from a fixed address or depot, such as certain transport workers, and building workers employed on a site for a long period, give the address of the depot, site or other fixed address.

(iii) For dock workers registered under the National Dock Labour Scheme who are in possession of a Pay Voucher Book issued by the National Dock Labour Board, give the address of the call stand or control point where they are required to prove attendance. For registered dock workers not issued with a Pay Voucher Book by the Board and other dock workers, give the name and address of the dock or wharf at which they are usually employed.

(iv) For seamen give the name of the ship and, if it is in the United Kingdom, the port in which it is lying, otherwise give the name of the home port.

Question 16

We now have the home address and the place of work on the census schedule. Those responsible for transport services and for traffic management need to measure the demand for these services, the travel modal-split (i.e. the share of the passenger traffic carried by each component the total transport system – trains, buses, cars, bicycles, etc.) and the load placed on each part of the road networks. Question 16 asks for the method of transport (the modal-split). To deal with changes of method during the journey (e.g. part of the way by train and part by bus) and certain special cases, the following notes were provided:

(i) For people using more than one method of transport to work give only the method by which the longest distance is travelled (for example if the normal journey to work is one mile by bus and five miles by train, write 'Train').

(ii) For people whose main method of transport to work is by bus, write either 'Public service bus' or 'Private bus' whichever is appropriate.

(iii) For people whose main method of transport to work is by motor cycle combination write 'Motor cycle combination' and not 'Motor cycle'.

(iv) For people who work at home write 'None'.

(v) For people with no fixed place of work give the method of transport most often used for going to work.

Question 17

In some countries where hours of work are short and/or wages low it is customary for workers to accept secondary employment in their spare time (often referred to colloquially as 'moonlighting'). As a result of a lowering of the average age at marriage at a time of relatively full employment there is probably an increasing tendency in Great Britain for workers to supplement their earnings by secondary employment though it is doubtful whether it is anything like the scale of such activity in Europe. Question 17 would measure the crude dimensions of this activity.[1] To have asked for specification of the nature of the secondary employment would have overloaded the census schedule. It would probably be more practical to use the census to identify areas of the country or strata of society where secondary employment is at a significant level and to pursue inquiries in these areas or strata by ad hoc survey. (This is one example of a situation in which it is advantageous for a permanent census organization to be equipped with its own field survey force.)

This concludes the questions relating to those who were employed during the reference period. We next have to investigate those who were not employed. There has always been the problem of reconciling the numbers returned at the census as unemployed with those counted as unemployed by the Department of Employment and Productivity. In the past the problem has been that the two concepts were quite different. In the census anyone who considered himself capable of work, i.e. as not 'retired' could describe himself as out of work even though he was not seriously seeking work or was too old or infirm to be fit to work. The Department of Employment and Productivity (until 1968, the Ministry of Labour) was and still is concerned with the more specific concept of a person registered at a local employment exchange as seeking work and the Department further distinguishes between those who are only temporarily laid off (and whose first need is for unemployment insurance benefit rather than

---

[1] Surprisingly the General Register Office state that 'current interest in identifying second jobs is not to identify patterns and trends in "moonlighting" but is to the end of reconciling Department of Employment and Productivity counts of jobs with the Census count of people'.

a new employer), those who are permanently unemployed and within the latter those who for various reasons must be regarded as unemployable.

Question 19

This question is designed to permit comparison between the census records and those of the Department of Employment and Productivity by seeking a specific reason for unemployment. It further enables separation to be made of the wholly retired, those who are prevented from working by sickness and those who may be active (e.g. home duties) but are not part of the labour force as normally defined for national productivity purposes.

Questions 20, 21

These questions are intended to identify, in respect of the unemployed or retired person, the occupation followed in his last full-time job and the identity within which that occupation was followed. It enables the total labour force, including the unemployed, to be classified by occupation. The unemployed person is likely to continue to follow his stated occupation (especially if skilled) on return to employment but he cannot be expected necessarily to return to the same industry. Therefore while he may be regarded, at the census, as having a current occupation, he has no current industry. The former industry is of little value as information in itself but asking for a statement of the name and business of the last employer pinpoints the last job and is a discipline which may help the respondent to provide a more reliable reply about his last occupation. He may otherwise claim as his previous occupation one which he followed for many years but did not in fact follow in his *last* employment.

9.28 RELIABILITY OF EMPLOYMENT INFORMATION

The arrangement of the employment questions in 1966 was

new and no detailed information is yet available of the quality of response. Some indication of the quality of response can, however, be obtained from the experience of the 1961 Census when the general coverage on employment was similar. The post-enumeration survey in 1961 indicated that economic position and economic status were generally reliably reported but comparison with Ministry of Labour statistics indicated a particular tendency for the census to understate part-time employment of married women. A full examination of the differences between census and the then Ministry of Labour statistics of the working population are given in the introductory notes to the 1961 occupation tables (General Register Office, 1966).

9.29 DESCRIPTION OF OCCUPATION

The statement of occupation is one of the most error-prone areas of the census schedule. The householder is required to offer virtually one-word descriptions of jobs the differentiation of which even for the limited purposes of census classification may require a number of words. The householder may omit a vital part of the occupation description either because he does not appreciate that they are vital (despite explanatory notes to the schedule and pre-census publicity) or because he does not know the full description; even the person described may not know the proper description of his job. As well as errors of omission, there are errors of commission. Everyone likes to put the best 'face' on his job and there has always been a tendency for people to describe their jobs in terms which suggest a higher status or skill than is, in fact, justified. Finally errors may be introduced in data-processing by the incorrect assignment of codes in the classification. This is especially likely if the classification is more refined than the data justify. It is possible then for a job description to be insufficiently specific to lead to one rubric. A choice of several equally applicable rubrics may be offered and an undesirable element of chance is introduced to the coding process which can only be controlled by establishing working conventions at a sufficiently early stage.

Neither manual inspection of the census schedule nor computer editing can reveal the errors if the occupation statement is consistent with all other particulars on the census schedule. A first attempt to measure the overall scale of error was made after the 1951 Census in Great Britain.

9.30 DEATH REGISTER MATCHING 1951

For persons who died sufficiently soon after the 1951 Census date to render a change of home address between enumeration and death unlikely, yet sufficiently long after the census to make it probable that they were enumerated at their usual home address and not in hospital, it was possible to match the census schedule and the information obtained at death registration in order to check the consistency of several comparable items of information and to gain some appreciation of the validity of such information. The procedure was as follows:

Information for each death registered in the period 1 to 7 May 1951, inclusive, was extracted on to a special form, the following particulars being noted:

(i) The registration district and sub-district.
(ii) Usual residence.
(iii) Name of deceased and, for children under age 16, the name of the parent.
(iv) Place of death.
(v) Sex, age, occupation code, cause of death code, marital condition and age of surviving spouse where applicable.
(vi) For married females, the year of last marriage and whether there were any children.

A search was then made among the census schedules of the appropriate enumeration district for the census entry, from which the following recorded details were extracted on to the same form:

(i) Age, marital condition.
(ii) Occupation code.
(iii) Age of surviving spouse.
(iv) For married females, year of last marriage and number of children.

A total of 9864 deaths were extracted and of these there were 892 for which the place of enumeration or circumstances at census date were such that the death entry did not furnish sufficient information to enable the census schedule to be traced (this number included 22 males and 17 females born since census day); there were also 449 cases where the schedule could be found but identification of the individual could not be made or was uncertain. There were a further 198 cases (111 males, 87 females) where a schedule was traced but the record indicated that the deaths related to infants born after the census day.

One of the principal objects of this matching operation was a test of discrepancy in occupational statement as between census schedule and death registration. Such a test was not only of interest as indicating possible tendencies to error in the completion of census schedules but was essential to proper assessment of the data used for the occupational mortality investigation carried out in connection with the census.

9.31 DISCREPANCY IN CLASS ASSIGNMENT

In the main the comparisons were restricted to the detection of differences in assignment to (i) the order, sub-order, or unit group of the occupation classification, (ii) social class or socio-economic group. For men complete agreement to unit occupational code (including those agreed as being unoccupied) was achieved for 56 per cent of the sample, falling from 67 per cent at ages 16–34 to 52 per cent at ages 75 and over;

some part of the total difference of 44 per cent was due to lack of any statement of occupation in one or other of the records – 12 per cent overall, varying from 7 per cent at ages 16–34 to 5 per cent at ages 60–64 and 18 per cent at ages 75 and over. For the more active ages 16–64, among 1349 for whom occupation was stated on both records, 139 (10 per cent) differed only in the unit number but 334 (25 per cent) disagreed even on the broader Order or Sub-order assignment; and only 876 (65 per cent) agreed in unit assignment. The discrepancy in social or socio-economic classification for men amounted to about one-fifth in all age-groups, being naturally rather larger for the finer breakdown of socio-economic groups than for the five broad social classes, but not to any very marked extent.

For women the occupational comparison was restricted to single women, where their own occupation was compared, and married women, where the occupation of the husband was compared since this only was recorded at death registration. No comparison was made for widows since their late husband's occupation would appear on the death record and he would not have appeared in the census enumeration. For married women the discrepancies in husband's occupations were, as might be expected, generally of the same order as for men. For single women's own occupations the main discrepancy was the failure to state any occupation on one or other of the two records compared, other types of discrepancy being relatively infrequent; indeed for the 133 single women under age 65 for whom an occupation was stated on both records, 100 or 75 per cent agreed down to the unit occupational classification.

9.32 ORDERS AND SUB-ORDERS OF THE CLASSIFICATION

In view of the similarity between the results for men and married women (husband's occupation) and the small number of single women in the sample, further analysis was confined to the men. While there was a considerable spread in the incidence of the discrepancies, it is noteworthy that concentrations were associated with Orders II (Agriculture), III (Mining), VI (Engineering) (especially Suborders VI.10 (Fitters) and VI. 18 (Electric welders, filers, press workers, steel erectors, etc.)), XIV (Building and contracting), XVI (Administrators, directors, managers), XVII (Transport), XVIII (Commercial occupations), XXII (Personal service), XXIII (Clerks), XXIV (Warehousemen) and XXVI (Unskilled occupations not elsewhere specified).

The sample was not sufficiently large to justify firm estimates of the likely net discrepancies in the relationship between the census data as a whole and the registered deaths which are brought into occupational mortality investigations, but at ages 16–64 (for which mortality indices are calculated) it seemed unlikely that the net discrepancy would exceed 10 per cent in any Order except Order XVI where the discrepancy might well be greater since, as indicated below, the assignment is dependent upon the mention of managerial status.

The difficulty with Orders II and XIV appeared to arise from the possibility that a relatively unskilled labourer might at one time be employed in agriculture and at another time be employed in building or in some unspecified occupation assigned to Order XXVI. There might also be some interchange between Order II and Order XXII, for example when a man was described at one time as a 'jobbing gardener' and at another as 'handyman domestic'.

There appeared to be a tendency for miners who had taken up unskilled employment in other occupations (assignable to Order XXVI), to be described at death as if they had remained engaged in mining.

'Fitter' is a notoriously vague description and (to quote an actual example) one had only to change the description from

'Fitter, cement works' to 'Under-general foreman, cement work' to a different Order assignment. Other actual examples were:

Census description	Order	Unit	Death registration	Order	Unit
Mechanical engineer (retired)	VI	183	Engineer's Draughtsman (retired)	XIX	799
Engineering	VI	183	Consulting Marine Engineer (retired)	XIX	787
Fitter engineer (retired)	VI	183	Electrician, torpedo works (retired)	VI	242
Railway signal fitter	VI	188	Platelayer (retired)	XIV	593
Engineer (retired)	VI	183	Ship's engineer	XVII	674

In this group, as elsewhere, some of the discrepancies were probably due to change of occupation being recorded on one document but not on the other, e.g. one man was recorded as 'Fitter (retired)' at the census and as 'Master photographer' on death registration.

There was a lack of agreement in Sub-order VI. 18 (other skilled workers in metal manufacture and engineering) where there were discrepancies within the Order, such as 'Retired locksmith' (census) contrasting with 'Retired master whitesmith' (death) or 'Press operator (retired)' (census) contrasting with 'Mechanic R.S.A.F.' (death), but also discrepancies between Orders such as 'Rigger ship repairers (retired)' (census) contrasting with 'Ship's rigger' (death), and 'Manufacturer of steel tube fittings (own account)' (census) altered to 'Company director, tube fitting works' (death).

Assignment to Order XVI was dependent on the mention of the status of 'Manager'. As an example, there may be quoted the case of a man who described himself at the census as 'Electrical engineer, retired' (Order VI, unit 241) and who was described at death registration as 'Manager, electrical engineers, retired' (Order XVI, unit 622).

Assignment to Order XVII was dependent on a sufficiently clear reference to transport itself and to a skill peculiar to a form of transport. (It has to be borne in mind that the occupational code is distinct from the industry classification and groups together similar occupations, e.g. clerks, regardless of the industry in which the clerks are engaged.) Examples of discrepancy were:

Census description	Order	Unit	Death registration	Order	Unit
Ganger, wharf	XVII	672	Dock clerk	XXIII	890
Coach proprietor	XVII	657	Retired coal merchant	XVIII	729
Carter, retired	XVII	654	Agricultural labourer	II	019
General manager, coal wharf	XVII	672	Coal office clerk	XXIII	890
Riveter's labourer, ship repair	VI	163	Seaman M.N.	XVII	675

Men who at one time followed a trade and at other times engaged in shopkeeping on their own account were involved in discrepancies in Order XVIII. If the retail business succeeded, the man might yet record his earlier trade skill at the census while at his death his widow may claim the status of a proprietor for him (or vice versa); if the venture failed the man might claim at the census to be a retired proprietor while on his death his widow may record the occupation in which the husband was last engaged (or vice versa). Sometimes there is a sheer discrepancy in description, e.g. 'Confectioner' (Order X, unit 422) contrasted with 'Confectionery Manufacturer' (Order XVI, unit 629).

Examples of discrepancies in Order XVIII were:

Census description	Order	Unit	Death registration	Order	Unit
Minister of religion (retired)	XIX	762	Retired grocer's carter (retired)	XVIII	741
Grocer, own account (retired)	XVIII	720	Tram conductor (retired)	XVII	661
General labourer	XXVI	950	Confectioner, tobacconist	XVIII	726
Sales manager, general engineers	XVIII	713	Planning engineer	XVI	622
Buyer (retired)	XVIII	712	Pastrycook, journeyman	X	422

Discrepancies might occur in Order XXII if (as in the example quoted under Order II) the description of a domestic servant, such as a handyman, referred to some particular current or former skill. Another example noted was that of a retired Army officer who was recorded on the census schedule, but not in the death entry, as a boarding-house keeper. The assignment of a cook or waiter could be changed from Order XXII to Order XVII if mention were made, in one record but not in the other, of his having been currently engaged in sea transport.

Men following occupations which involve some clerical duties, e.g. agents, canvassers, warehousemen, storekeepers, dock officials, may be incorrectly described as 'clerks', in which case they are assigned to Order XXIII. (See example above under Order XVII.) The converse error also occurs. Such discrepancies commonly affect Orders XVII (Transport), XVIII (Commercial, financial, etc., occupations), though this order expressly excludes clerical staff, and XXIV (Warehousemen, etc).

Order XXVI comprises unskilled occupations not classified to other orders and thus any lack of specificity on either document may mean assignment to this order while an entirely different order is used for coding the other record. There are also genuine changes in occupation which may be noted on one record but not on the other. (See the general labourer/confectioner, tobacconist contrast noted above.)

This brief review covers only the discrepancies involving a change of Order or Sub-order; local discrepancies involving only the unit number are liable to occur from slight changes or extension in description, e.g. Seaman = 675, Donkeyman on steam vessel = 677; or Coal miner, lampman = 047, Colliery lampman (above ground) = 049. The scope for such minor discrepancies is wide in such a detailed classification but as they operate less from deliberation than from chance rearrangements in description, the net error is probably smaller than the gross displacements. Some of the discrepancies were due to differences in coding but in a random selection of 300 discrepancies which were examined in detail only twenty-two cases were found where the discrepancy in unit number arose from differences in interpretation of the classification.

9.33 THE NET EFFECT UPON SOCIO-ECONOMIC DISTRIBUTIONS

The matching test was also designed to measure the net effect of discrepancies on the social class and socio-economic group distributions. At the ages 20–64 which are mainly of interest in relation to occupational mortality or other social studies (since the distributions here broadly relate to current occupations), there was a slight upward shift in social class at death registration. Social Class I and II comprised 16·0 per cent at census and 17·9 per cent at death, the Social Class III proportion was virtually unchanged, Social Classes IV and V comprised 36·8 per cent at census and 35·2 per cent at death. This was a very small net shift. At the working ages the net shift at death in socio-economic group was also generally upward in status, but the effect on the shape of the distribution was very small; groups 1 to 4, 8 and 13 (farmers, agricultural workers, personal service, administrative, professional and managerial, Armed Forces) gained slightly at the expense of group 7, 11 and 12 (shop assistants, semi-skilled and unskilled workers).

At ages 65 and over the gross discrepancies were greater as a result of the greater opportunities for discrepancy in occupational description but the net upward shift in social class and socio-economic group was smaller. Social Class I and II comprised 21·4 per cent at census and 22·1 per cent at death registration. This compared with an increase from 16·0 to 17·9 per cent for ages 20–64. The reduction in Socio-economic Groups 11 and 12 (semi-skilled and unskilled workers) at death registration as compared with the census record at ages 65 and over was only from 25·0 per cent to 24·1 per cent compared with a reduction from 32·5 per cent to 30·2 per cent at ages 20–64.

In summary it may be said that, while the occupational classification sometimes fell victim to the combined forces of its own specificity and the human capacity for variation in description, the general impression emerged that the level of reliability of occupational assignment at the census justified the statistical analyses which were based thereon. While discrepancies between census and death records were sometimes favourable and sometimes unfavourable to the status of the deceased, there was on balance a tendency for the social standing of a group to be slightly raised on the basis of death registration as compared with the census. It seemed likely that, though both the deceased, at the census, and their widows (or other informants), at death registration, tend to use flattering descriptions of recent employment or to select an earlier occupation if this appeared to them of greater weight, there was rather less inaccuracy of this kind at the census, surrounded as it was with an atmosphere of fact-finding and of legal persuasion, and conducted with more publicity and instructional assistance than is death registration. The shift in socio-economic distribution was not sufficiently serious to threaten the validity of the occupational mortality analyses.

Nevertheless it was considered that undue specificity in the 1951 occupation classification made coding vulnerable to the chance inclusion or exclusion of supplementary words in job description and accordingly the 1961 classification was reduced to 200 units as compared with 600 in the 1951 classification.

9.34 POST-ENUMERATION SURVEY 1961

In the post-enumeration survey the questions relating to occupation began, as in the census itself, by asking for a single term and then asked for a verbal description of the work done. This was supplemented by a series of check lists for different types of worker, the check lists giving broad groups into which such workers could be classified. For example, the interviewer had to obtain enough information to decide whether a non-manual worker was professional, technical, managerial, clerical or in some other category. The final two questions in the occupation section of the survey attempted to relate the person concerned to the group with whom he worked. He was asked for the title of his immediate supervisor and those who were foremen, managers or supervisors were asked to state the type of work that they supervised (this was a check on inflation of status). The survey therefore provided a test of the accuracy likely to be achieved in a single term job description though the test was necessarily blunted by the intervention of other sources of divergence – different respondents may have been involved, the same respondent may have replied at different levels of accuracy on the two occasions and the data processing arrangements, especially the occupation coding, were more strictly controlled for the post-enumeration survey than for the census itself which was on a massive scale.

Some 5,000 economically active and retired men were included in the post-enumeration survey. There was agreement in the assignment to a rubric of the occupation classification in 92 per cent of cases. Among those whose assignment to an occupation unit differed between the census and the post-enumeration survey, 35 per cent were assigned to the same occupation order but to different units within that order; the remainder were assigned to different occupation orders.

9.35 DEATH MATCHING 1961

As in 1951 a comparison of census and death registration records was carried out for a sample of those dying soon after the 1961 Census. A total of 2196 males were matched and of these 1390 (63 per cent) were assigned to the same occupation unit at death registration and at the census. Among the discrepancies nearly three in ten were assigned to different units within the same order and seven in ten to different orders. This was a disturbingly low level of agreement. A hard core of discrepancies was represented by (a) those cases where the two statements, at census and death respectively, appeared to relate to jobs with no apparent connection (A 'collector, Gas Board' at death registration had been enumerated as 'painter and decorator'), (b) those where two different jobs were described though they were related, e.g. by being within the same industry. This kind of discrepancy is likely to arise when a man changes to a less exacting job with advancing age or illness; he may describe his current occupation at the census and, on death, his widow may describe the occupation he followed during most of his working life (or it may be the other way round). The nature of these discrepancies suggests that because of the possibility of a different approach by the two different informants (the man himself at the census, a relative at death), death registration records are not a wholly valid check of the accuracy of census statements. The poor results from this death-matching exercise should not, therefore, detract from the general impression from the 1961 post-enumeration survey that the reduction in the specificity of the occupation classification in 1961 as compared with 1951 did improve the accuracy of the statistical distributions of occupation.

It is likely that the better structured form of the questions in 1966 led to a further improvement in the reliability of the occupational assignments.

9.36 INDUSTRY – ERRORS IN STATEMENTS
The use of the name, address, and business of the employer as a reference to an already industrially classified register of establishments must reduce error of response to a very low level. The 1961 post-enumeration survey found the level of agreement to be 99 per cent.

9.37 HOURS WORKED BY PART-TIME WORKERS
A check on the recording of hours worked by part-time workers was made in the 1961 post-enumeration survey but it was confined to women since part-time working was, at that time and probably still is, predominantly a characteristic of the employment of women. The number of hours was confirmed for 83 per cent of all the women originally returned as part-time workers. Some of those who originally claimed to be working part-time were shown by the post-enumeration survey to be working full-time.

9.38 DEPENDENCY
In keeping with the increasing economic emphasis in demography attention has to be given to the classification of the population according to their mode of participation in the

economy. A simple classification by type of economic activity can be drawn up as follows:

A. Economically active population:
   1. Employed.
   2. Unemployed.

B. Inactive population:
   1. With income
      (i) Former members of active population (i.e. pensioners deriving their subsistence from former activity).
      (ii) Living on income from capital, State aid, etc.
   2. Without income, dependents
      (i) Students.
      (ii) Home houseworkers.
      (iii) Persons in institutions.
      (iv) Other adults in the home.

Since it is the active population who provide the goods and services which are consumed by all, it is an important part of long-term economic planning, especially in relation to social security, to assess, from a total population point of view, the likely trend in the numerical relationship between the inactive and active populations.

The same kind of study is of importance at the household and more particularly at the family level for the purpose of measuring the economic strength of different structures. The problem is to attach the dependent members of the family to the member or members upon whom they are dependent. The supporters may be further classified to show not only the numbers of their dependents but also the sector of economy or branch of economic activity on which they, the supporters, are in turn dependent.

It is important to note that the analyses of household and family structure, and of dependency are problems of arrangement of data already on the census schedule; they do not involve specific questions except that, in the case of dependency, a question is needed to identify income recipients.

9.39 INCOME

As distinct from analyses of dependency which are concerned with the presence or absence of incomes, there has been little development, within the population census in Great Britain, in the direction of analysing incomes by size. As a result it has been necessary in the study of levels of living to turn to a battery of indicators such as food consumption, infant mortality, education facilities. Some countries have carried out household income and expenditure surveys on an ad hoc basis but not as part of the population census, so that it is only possible to cross-tabulate with a limited number of other social and economic characteristics and thus to assess the value of these characteristics as proxies for income. It has to be borne in mind that household budget inquiries of the continuous sample survey type (e.g. the British National Family Expenditure Survey) provide constantly up-to-date information in circumstances of prices and wages which are always changing and for this reason it has been argued that there is a strong balance of advantage in favour of the survey method. However, while this balance of advantage may apply to the measure of national trends in prices and incomes it does not dispose of the case for a question on income in the national census.

It is well understood that the census is a measure of population characteristics at a point of time. Though it is true that the value of money tends to change more rapidly than the other variables measured, the obsolescence argument applies to all census data. This argument is weakened by the fact that censuses now tend to take place more frequently than they used. In any case, since it is the value of money which is changing, the relativities of income (the real focus of interest) which are affected only by the pressures of the labour market and differentials in the timing and success of wage bargaining in different trades, are less changeable.

While a continuous sample survey is adequate to measure broad national changes in income, such a survey is never likely to be large enough to permit the examination of local differentials. The National Family Expenditure Survey is barely sufficient in size to give reliable indications of differences between standard regions. There is a real need, for planning purposes, to examine incomes in local authority areas.

The main argument for an income question in the census is the need to understand the relationship between income and housing, family size, education, occupation and other characteristics as a basis for projecting the demand for services and forecasting the likely social effects of changes in the relative affluence of different strata of the population, in different localities.

While the British lack of candour about incomes dies hard, especially where the tax authorities are concerned, public antipathy to questions about income is very much weaker than it used to be. Statements of income are required for so many purposes (education grants, house mortgages, etc., as well as income tax), that a request for such a statement no longer occasions outraged surprise. Reference to a 'means test' has much less of an emotive ring than it used to have.

Nevertheless there must be constraints. A census authority seeking information about incomes must take even greater care to demonstrate than census records are confidential and that the information cannot be passed on to a third party. It will get a better response if it avoids making a direct request for precise details of means (no one likes being pinned down to an exact amount) but rather offers the respondent the opportunity to classify himself within reasonably broad income brackets.

In the 1968 pretest for the 1971 Census of Great Britain

the following question was asked in respect of persons aged 15 and over:

> Write the person's income during the last twelve months from each of the following. If none, write 'None'.
>
> (a) Wages, salary, bonus, commission or tips from all jobs, *before* deduction of tax, etc.
>
> (b) Profits from trade, business, or profession, *after* deduction of capital allowances, but *before* deduction of tax.
>
> (c) Any other source (*before* deduction of tax where applicable) for example, retirement, old age and widow's pensions; other State benefits, occupational pensions, annuities, rent from property, interest and dividends; education grants, etc. Do *not* include capital receipts.
>
> THIS INFORMATION IS NOT REQUIRED FOR ANY PURPOSE CONNECTED WITH TAX ASSESSMENT.

Although full explanatory notes were added and despite the disclaimer about tax assessment, the response was not satisfactory. This was probably because exact amounts were asked for rather than classification within a band. A later pre-test in 1969 was restricted to broad bands of income but the results are not yet available.

It may be added that if exact amounts are required it is a good plan to ask for the *net* income and to ask separately for the deductions item by item (tax, social security contribution, etc.).

9.40 EDUCATION

An important development in the population census has been the progress from a mere assessment of literacy to a study of standards of instruction attained and even to a survey of the acquirement of university degrees and diplomas and technological qualifications. This development, of course, mirrors the economic progress of the world and the rise in educational standards which this economic progress has enforced.

The extent to which education and employment are

correctly matched is of immense importance to the attainment of high levels of productivity; this is why there has been a growing interest in scientific and technological qualifications.

Definition of standards of instruction must inevitably be in terms of the administration of the educational system of the country concerned, and they will probably only have application within the context of that system. The analyses then take the form of cross-tabulations of standards of instruction with occupation (especially age of entry into the occupation), branch of economic activity, status, socio-economic group, and with other characteristics such as housing, family structure, and fertility.

It has to be borne in mind that in Great Britain all primary, secondary and higher educational services are under the direct control or the supervision of central and local government. The Department of Education and Science is able, as a by-product of administration, to compile and publish comprehensive and detailed statistics of activity *within* the educational institutions. The population census is not therefore the natural vehicle for inquiries about such activity. In the 1966 Census of Great Britain it was necessary therefore to ask only two questions which could not be answered from within the education system itself. First a population based question to establish the extent of full-time attendance at an educational establishment beyond the age at which such attendance ceased to be compulsory (i.e. age 15). Second a question to establish the extent to which the population in particular age groups (and occupations) possessed degrees, diplomas and other qualifications. These questions were:

22. Will the person be a student attending full-time at an educational establishment during the next term? (See Notes.) Write 'Yes' or 'No'.

For people aged 18 and over

23. (a) Has the person obtained any degrees, diplomas, associateships or other professional or vocational qualifications after attaining the age of 18? (See Notes.) Write 'Yes' or 'No' at I.

(b) If 'Yes' state at II all such qualifications obtained, followed by the major subject or group of subjects in which each was obtained. (See Notes.)

The reference to 'next term' arises from the fact that the census was taken at a time when many educational establishments were closed for the Easter vacation; a reference to 'now' would have been at risk of variable interpretation.

Question 23 was mainly directed to measuring the overall pool of scientific manpower; it had to be framed in the widest possible terms despite the heavier data processing involved in order that no relevent qualification should be missed.

9.41 STRUCTURE OF CENSUS ANALYSES

The main structure of census analyses can be set out systematically as follows:

UNITS	AXES
Person	Sex, age, marital condition, fertility, birthplace, nationality, education, economic activity, occupation, industry, workplace, migration.
Family	Structural type, situation in household, economic strength (ratio of economically active to dependent members).
Household	Structural type, family content, economic strength, characteristics of chief economic supporter, housing.
Locality (cluster)	Size, industrial character, urban/rural division, function.
Administrative area	Principal aggregate of tabulation.

9.42 ADMINISTRATIVE AREAS

These are as follows:

England and Wales

The country is split into 58 Administrative Counties and the area of the Greater London Council (which subsumes the areas of the former counties of London and Middlesex). Within these Administrative Counties there are 82 County Boroughs of the same general status as the counties; their populations normally form entirely separate statistical units except that in certain census tabulations the 'administrative counties and their associated county boroughs' are used as divisions of the total populations.

Within Greater London there are 32 London Boroughs and the City of London. Within the administrative counties there are (1) 270 Municipal Boroughs; (2) 535 Urban Districts; Some urban areas are divided into wards for local electoral purposes. (3) 473 Rural Districts; (4) Within Rural districts, the 11,162 Civil Parishes. These areas appear in some census tables but do not appear in the normal tabulations of vital statistics.

Scotland

There are 33 Counties. Within these Counties there are (1) 4 Counties of cities (Aberdeen, Dundee, Glasgow, Edinburgh); these like the county boroughs in England and Wales have the same status as counties; (2) 20 Large Burghs (similar to municipal boroughs in England and Wales); (3) 176 Small Burghs (equivalent to urban district councils in England and Wales); (4) 198 Nonburghal towns and villages. These have no legally defined areas and are identified only in census tabulations. Some of these towns have populations greater than that of many of the Burghs, and many occur within the central industrial belt of the country. It has been customary to regard those with a population of 1000 or more as urban but this is an arbitrary distinction; (5) 869 Civil Parishes. As in England and Wales these do not figure in the normal tabulations of vital statistics though their populations are given in census tables.

England and Wales

Aggregates. For summary purposes the country has been divided into 9 Standard Regions each comprising several counties or parts of counties including associated county boroughs. This enables a broad examination to be made of geographical differentials and of the influence of the higher industrialization of the northern areas, and of the more agricultural and rural character of Eastern and South-Western areas. For the study of urban and population density effects, the local authority units are aggregated as:

Conurbations.

Outside conurbations.

Urban areas with populations of 100,000 or more.

Urban areas with populations of 50,000 and under 100,000.

Urban areas with populations under 50,000.

Rural districts.

10. *Organization of the Census*

10.1 TIMING

The census is taken on a particular day, at intervals of several years, and endeavours to count a population which is not only continually changing in total size, but is also changing in constitution (age, sex, occupation, etc.) and in its geographical disposition within the national boundary. In times of industrial crisis or of mobilization of military forces, violent changes may be taking place; on a minor level, sharp changes in regional distribution occur in the usual holiday seasons. It would be ideal therefore to fix a time at which such changes are minimal, so that on the one hand the actual enumeration may be facilitated by stable conditions, and on the other the results may be more likely to reflect the average condition of the population about the time of the census, i.e. the census will be representative of that era and intercensal changes will typify broad trends rather than sharp and often transient fluctuations. Choice of census year is largely determined, however, by considerations of continuity and regularity, such as the desirability of maintaining equal decennial intervals from the first census in Britain in 1801.

In any particular year the day chosen should be such as to find most people at their usual occupation and in their usual residence, so as to narrow the gap between de facto and de jure enumerations. While it is desirable to choose a week-end out of the holiday season so as to minimize absences from home for holiday, social, or business reasons, it is also desirable to carry out the enumeration at a time of the year when the weather is not inclement and the evenings are light so as to facilitate the task of the enumerators. There are statistical advantages in choosing a date near the middle of the year so that little adjustment is needed to produce a mid-year estimate. In Britain the choice of a Sunday in April is a compromise which attempts to take account of all these considerations.

If, as in some countries, the enumeration is spread over a period of weeks rather than made on a single day, certain problems are created. Some persons who move during the enumeration period may be missed altogether, since the area in which they originally lived may not be canvassed before they move and enumeration may be completed in the area of their new home by the time they arrive; there is equally the possibility of double enumeration. Furthermore, enumerators tend to ignore the nominal date of enumeration and to record information as at the date of the visit; in spite of instructions it is found that some infants are included in the census though born after the census date, and some persons who died after the census are excluded. The fact that in Britain a householder completes the schedule, instead of giving answers to an interviewer, enables a simultaneous count to be taken in all parts of the country on a single day and thus largely avoids these difficulties.

10.2 ENUMERATION DISTRICTS

The method of enumeration in Great Britain is basically simple though the administrative task is very large. The country is split up into districts the boundaries of which are carefully defined on maps and the area of which can be covered from dwelling to dwelling by the enumerator within two days at most. These districts are sub-divisions of registration districts and local registration staff traditionally become supervising census officers for the duration of the enumeration; by the same token enumeration districts automatically add up to local authority areas. Certain special enumeration districts are created where an institution (e.g. a hospital) is large enough to constitute an enumeration district in itself. This mapping process requires a meticulous approach and thorough consultation with local authority staff (e.g. planning officers) who are familiar with the local territory and with developments that have taken place since the last census. The object is to present the enumerator with boundaries to his district which are unambiguous and are easily recognized from the ground. A railway cutting or an open space are clear boundaries; a boundary which cuts across the middle of a street (i.e. depends on remembering to stop at a particular house number) is less satisfactory. There should be no 'no-man's-land' which is in doubt between one enumerator and another.

Questionnaires (schedules) to be completed by the house-holder are distributed a few days before census day and are collected as quickly as possible after that date, a large proportion on the day following census day. Enumerators are briefed and are equipped with instruction manuals to enable them to identify separate dwellings and households and to deal with difficulties of interpretation of the schedule. Enumerators check that the schedules are complete and pass them on to the local census officers who inspect them again before transmitting them to census headquarters for data processing.

10.3 TRAINING OF ENUMERATORS AND CENSUS OFFICERS

As already indicated, in Great Britain the principal census officers in the field are the local registrars of births and deaths. Their role is a vital one since in any survey the field work is the stage in the operation at which headquarters control becomes tenuous and everything depends upon local super-vision. It is important therefore that the local registrars who are diverted to this task should have a good understanding of the objectives and machinery of the population census (just as it is essential for the production of high-quality vital statistics that their normal registration duties should be carried out with an understanding of the methodology and purposes of registration systems). It is unfortunate that hitherto the registrars of births and deaths have not been required as needing to be professional officers though they have had to be given, with little preparation, not only the task of supervising the field work but also the task of recruiting and training the enumerators. An Institute of Population Registration has now been formed as a body to train and

examine its members in all techniques of population registration including census-taking. It is hoped that this will do
much to ensure the supply of manpower of the right calibre.
There is the further difficulty that the registration officers
cannot at present be deployed for sufficiently long to devote
enough time and attention to the enumeration. It may be
necessary to redefine the duties of local registration staff and
to increase their numbers so that there can be a corps of
census intelligence officers permanently allocated to census
organization.

A census authority needs to have close and continuing
contact with the field. There are a number of reasons for this.
Under present conditions the normal requirements of pre-
census planning surveys for testing the mapping of districts,
the questionnaire design and the mechanics of sampling and
enumeration are difficult to fulfil. A survey of this kind has
perforce to be mounted as a special operation requiring
specific authority and money. There ought to be continuing
opportunities for experimentation with different sampling
frames, different arrangements for improving self-enumeration, different ways of designing enumeration districts, for
discovering the best way to ask questions, and for ascertaining
and advising on local data requirements. For sampling frame
development and for the design of enumeration districts there
is a need for close knowledge of building development,
changes of land use, and other industrial and population
changes in individual localities. There are a number of
operations in connexion with the validation of the census that
require further recourse in the field. There is a strong case for
a permanent local organization.

The more understanding of the census objectives the
local census officers bring to their task, the better will be the
effectiveness of their supervision and organization. They need
to be able to appreciate the difficulties in the reaction to
census questions which are likely to arise whether these

K*

difficulties arise from the scope of the question or from its form or from the concepts and definition. They must fully understand the requirements of any sampling scheme and be able to discipline the enumerators to follow the rules precisely. They ought also to appreciate the data processing arrangements and in relation to these, the deficiencies in schedule completion the prevention of which should be given the highest priority. These matters cannot be properly dealt with by treating the census as a temporary distraction from vital registration duties. (We return to this problem later.)

In Great Britain the population census is carried out 'on the cheap'. There are no canvassers or interviewers to elicit answers from members of the population; the householder enumerates his own household and writes down the answers to the questions. The 'enumerator' is mainly recruited part-time from students, clerks, teachers and local officials. Normally his duty is first to explore the area defined and mapped in his enumeration book, identify all buildings, identify those buildings or parts of buildings which are dwellings and the separate households within those dwellings, and deliver a census schedule to each household. He lists each household in his enumeration book (see later). This part of his duty is carried out in the week preceding the Sunday which is census day. In 1966 because this was the first census to be based entirely on a sample of the population the distribution of schedules was preceded by a distribution of explanatory leaflets.

The distribution of schedules is normally a spare-time activity since most of the enumerators have regular day-time employment. Census officers are recommended to recruit people who are free to give the whole of the Monday immediately following census day to their work so as to be able to collect the major proportion of the completed schedules on that day. The enumerator's instruction book for 1966 contained the following time-table:

Census Calendar

2–7 April	Saturday to Thursday	Deliver preliminary leaflets
12–21 April	Tuesday to Thursday	Deliver census forms
24 April	Sunday	Census day
25–28 April	Monday to Thursday	Collect census forms
9 May	Monday	Hand over completed material to census officer on or before this date

The instruction book was issued on recruitment several weeks before census day. After an interval during which the enumerator could have an opportunity to study the instruction book, the enumerators were called together by the census officer for training sessions. A census district for which each census officer was responsible covered 70–90 enumeration districts. The census officer would normally call the enumerators together in batches of twenty or so. Bearing in mind that the census officer during this time is continuing with his normal registration duties and that the enumerators are at work during the day, it is impracticable for the census officer to give one enumerator more than a single session of 1–2 hours. Such a session would consist of a short talk on general aims, a run through the instruction book to emphasize and expand on a number of points, and the provision of answers to specific questions raised by the enumerator. This is barely sufficient and underlines what has already been said about the need for a more continuing form of local organization.

10.4 THE ENUMERATOR'S INSTRUCTION BOOK

Some points from the instruction book have already been referred to during the discussion of census topics but it will be useful here to summarize the coverage of the book:

(1) A summary of duties and a time-table.

(2) A statement that an appointment card will be issued

showing the name of the enumerator and signed by the census officer and that is to be presented, on demand, as evidence of identity and authority.

(3) A statement stressing the confidential status of census records.

(4) Basic information relating to the concepts and definitions used in the census (building, household, rooms, dwelling, institutional premises) and where sampling is to be employed, the sampling procedure and the need to comply strictly with that procedure.

(5) A description of the enumeration record which the enumerator is required to complete. In 1966 in Great Britain this was ruled to take one line for each household with a column for each of the following items:

Address of dwelling.

Building type.

Name of head of household (or person in charge of institution). Part of building occupied (if a sharing household or a dwelling in an institution).

Number of rooms occupied by household (unless institution other than hotel or boarding-house).

(6) A description of the different kinds of census forms or schedules applicable to different situations, e.g. for 1966:

H for private households.

I for small institutions.

C for hotels.

F for H.M. Forces establishments.

L for large institutions (pre-listed by the census officer).

P for individual returns (any individual adult member of a household has the right to make a personal return if he does not wish to disclose details to the head of the household).

(7) Examples of how to complete the records in certain typical situations listed in (6) above, especially what to do with a caravan site.

(8) Instructions about collection of the schedules and about checking them for completeness; what to do about incomplete replies or refusals.

(9) Instructions about arranging and serial numbering of schedules.

(10) Instructions as to delivery of documents to census officer.

10.5 ENUMERATION OF SPECIAL CLASSES

Where security arrangements permit it is usual in Great Britain for Forces personnel, and their dependants living in married quarters within the boundaries of the Forces establishment, to be enumerated by local enumerators; where this is not possible, the responsibility for the enumeration is placed on the officer commanding the unit. The Admiralty undertakes the enumeration of all naval ships within Home station limits, the schedules being forwarded direct to census headquarters.

People on civilian ships are generally enumerated by officers of H.M. Customs and Excise on the kind of schedules used for collective establishments with slight modification to adapt them for use on ships. They *exclude* (*a*) vessels with no sleeping accommodation (*b*) ships of the U.K. or foreign navies (*c*) any ships which by arrangement are enumerated by the local census officer. They *include* any ship arriving in port within a prescribed time after census day (usually three weeks) which has not already been enumerated and which has been, at census midnight, (*a*) in a British port or anchorage, (*b*) voyaging between such ports or anchorage; or (*c*) on a fishing voyage without touching at a foreign port or a port of the Irish Republic.

Homeless people are dealt with by the police. Travellers

over census night are advised to get in touch with the local census officer of the area of their destination if they have not been enumerated before departure.

10.6 CENSUS OFFICERS

Apart from the recruiting, instructing and equipping of enumerators to which reference has already been made, the local census officers have important duties. They receive comprehensive written instructions from headquarters and are called together for briefing sessions conducted by headquarters (in 1966, three half days). They are required to report to headquarters just before census day that enumerators have been allocated to districts, have been supplied with all necessary forms and records and that all local arrangements are proceeding satisfactorily.

During enumeration the census officer's main duty is to be available in his office to deal with any difficulties (sickness of enumerators or failure, for other reasons, to carry out duties; difficulties between enumerators and the public).

After census day the census officer must satisfy himself that collection of schedules is proceeding rapidly and should obtain reports from enumerators when the process has been completed.

When the completed schedules and records books have been received from the enumerators, these must be checked for completeness and for apparent errors. Area coding of address of usual residence may be delegated to the census officer on the grounds that his local knowledge will enable him to locate the local authority assignment more easily than headquarters staff. He may be required to make certain specific local inquiries, e.g. in connection with households entirely absent on census night, from their usual address. Finally he must dispatch the schedules to the headquarters processing office. (For England and Wales this is, at present, at Titchfield, Hampshire.)

11. *Data-processing*

11.1 SCHEDULE REVISION

The data-processing of a national population census even if conducted entirely on a sample basis, is a massive task involving millions of individual records. A carefully planned and systematic organization is essential.

The first stage is usually described in Great Britain as schedule revision. This is the first stage at which some improvement of the original census data can be effected, though it is not the function of this operation to correct faults in general. This correction is left to the editing stage. It consists of inspection of the schedules and enumeration record books in order to ensure that all information, already in numerical form, from which direct punching takes place is complete and in the correct form.

Where information is missing, other information on the schedule may be referred to as a basis for estimating the missing items. For example the age of a married man, if missing, can be assumed, in Great Britain, to be three years older than the wife (or a wife, three years younger than the husband). A child enumerated with the parents may be assumed to have been born two years after the date of marriage. A missing age left unassumed will be picked up at the editing stage. Marital condition is another of the missing items commonly assumed. Where age is missing and cannot be assumed from other schedule data a random selection can be made from a typical population distribution.

Some obvious incorrect or unacceptable answers to questions can be corrected. For example the only acceptable entries against the various household amenities are 'sole use', 'shared' or 'none'. If 'yes' is entered this may be safely altered to 'sole use'. 'No' may be taken as 'none'. If no entries are made, it can be assumed that the dwelling is similar to other dwellings in the same street or block of flats.

It is usual to treat a person described as 'bedsitter' or as a 'tenant' either as part of the private household or as a separate one-person household according to other circumstances.

Omission of any entry against 'number of live-born children' is usually regarded as indicating zero unless children are enumerated on the same schedule.

There is sometimes doubt about the purpose served by an institution housing a collective or non-private household, and it is advisable to prepare from local information or obtain from the appropriate Central Government Department, lists of institutions already classified by usage and indicating their normal occupation. It is often necessary during schedule revision to transfer households from the private category to the non-private category and vice versa. For example in 1966 a private household with five or more persons described as boarders, foster children, lodgers, patients, employees, etc., was, by convention, transferred to the non-private category.

11.2 CODING AND PUNCHING

Coding is the translation of words into numbers or more correctly the translation of verbally classifiable information into the appropriate rubrics of that classification. Errors can be introduced at this stage. Even if frank errors are not committed, there is a subjective element in the operation and the opportunity for variation in interpretation of the verbal information from one coder to another. It has to be borne in mind that a very large number of coders are normally involved and that much of the census coding refers to extensive classification; this is especially true of occupation and area coding.

Instead of having to train coders afresh at each census it is, therefore, highly desirable to maintain from one census to another a permanent cadre, or at least a nucleus, of skilled coders in these fields. It is also imperative to build up dictionaries so that uncommon descriptions can be given a standard allocation to a code rubric instead of being dealt with on each occasion as a new and possibly variant decision. Coding must be reproducible, i.e. allocation to a rubric must be reversible when information is retrieved. To put it another way, the title of a rubric must have a specific relationship to its contents.

Quality control procedures can be introduced. In the 1961 Census of Great Britain the basic system was to divide the work into lots of predetermined size and to check each lot fully until the error rate fell below a specified percentage x. When the error rate had fallen to below this level, subsequent lots were checked on a sample basis as long as the error rate remained below y per cent, where y exceeded x by a suitable margin of tolerance. If the error rate rose above y per cent full checking was reintroduced until the error rate again fell below x per cent. Such a system greatly reduces the burden of checking.

Errors can also be introduced in card punching, the most important type of error being the transposition of digits in a code thus transferring a unit from the correct category to an incorrect one. Quality control procedures can be applied to punching in the same way as described above for coding.

The long-term objective will be to make coding and punching as automatic as possible. The dilemma facing the census authority is that the technical means to achieve automatic coding and punching have been developed but their efficient use is dependent on the introduction of more skilled manpower at the enumeration stage thus considerably raising the cost of the whole operation, since this is the most costly stage. Lectors are available which will 'read' marks against digits or special script on a form or schedule and punch cards automatically. While the lectors can be designed to select dominant marks and to tolerate some latitude in their position on the form, the marking of the document does require a minimal amount of skill and it is doubtful if this can yet be generally expected of householders. Thus mark sensing could, at present, be introduced in Great Britain only at the cost of abandoning self-enumeration and introducing a much more expensive canvass system. It is possible also that, for example, common job descriptions could be read by the computer and compared with a stored dictionary to translate them into number codes which could be automatically recorded on the personal data tape, leaving only a small fraction of more difficult or more ambiguous descriptions to be coded manually. With present procedures this would not only involve more supervision of the completion of schedules so that householders could be guided towards the commoner terms of descriptions, but it would also involve a good deal of alpha-numeric punching. The cost-benefit equation currently leads to acceptance of the present drudgery of manual coding and punching. However, the equation ought to be continually tested.

11.3 EDITING

In order to make the most efficient use of the computer it is essential to take advantage of its capacity for producing a clean input by editing the crude data and indicating discrepancies for correction. The procedure is to list as many incongruities as can be foreseen as possible, and therefore as requiring to be eliminated. The computer is then programmed to read the initial data tape, to seek and recognize these incongruities and either to print out details of the indicator units for reference back to the schedules or to follow prescribed conventions for corrective action. (It should be understood that all this is in addition to and not in substitution for (i) a manual inspection of the schedules prior to punching, and (ii) normal computer checks for recognition of presence of codes, etc.)

It is unnecessary to list all the possible incongruities here but a few examples can be given:

Household occupies whole dwelling but shares a particular amenity. This is a *valid doubt*. If reference back to the records indicates that the dwelling is the only dwelling in the building this is clearly a fault. If it is not a single dwelling in a building the schedule statement may be compared with schedules for neighbouring dwellings to see whether this is presumptive evidence of the other sharer. In general the schedule has to be accepted as correct unless there is some real evidence to the contrary.

Aged under 16 at marriage. This usually arises from indistinct or impossible dates of marriage being entered. They can either be corrected after closer inspection of the schedule or by a random selection from a distribution of marriage ages appropriate to other details recorded on the schedule.

Age over x (where x is an advanced age known to be rarely exceeded in the population). It is necessary to apply a check at an upper limit because of the risk that an error has arisen from a simple transposition of digits in punching, e.g. 59 being punched as 95, and also because an error at these advanced ages where numbers are small is relatively more serious than at younger ages where numbers are large.

Occupation/industry/status. The number of acceptable combinations of occupation and industry for a person with a given employment status is often large but nevertheless limited. It is feasible, with the assistance of advice from industry and appropriate Government department, to construct a matrix of the acceptable combinations and to edit out, as a doubt, any combination which cannot be found in the matrix.

Apart from the resulting improvement in the data the edited computer runs are not wasted as it is often possible to use them to obtain useful preliminary and provisional counts of characteristics that may be urgently required.

11.4 TABULATIONS

It has already been emphasized that the whole organization of the census should be constructed on the basis of the ultimate uses of the data expressed as possible in specific tabular terms. Wherever possible an indication of these uses has been given in Section 9 when discussing census topics. The non-specific extraction of piles of computer output based on a cross-tabulation of every combination of census characteristics would be a negation of design and utterly wasteful; nor is there any point in laying down recommendations for standard tabulations except for the restricted purposes of international comparability in certain *published* tabulations. For this latter purpose the U.N. recommendations are set out in 'Principles and Recommendations for the 1970 Population Censuses' and in 'Principles and Recommendations for the 1970 Housing Censuses' (U.N. 1969).

Given this flexibility and the compact data storage facility of the computer it is no longer necessary for a census authority to plan almost wholly in terms of a publication programme and to regard ad hoc tabulations as exceptional and a matter for a deferred programme of post-censal analysis. This was the pre-computer tradition. In this era in Great Britain the publication programme represented an enforced 'package' for all consumers; thoughtfully and painstakingly designed to meet most requirements but not in fact tailored to any individual customer (in those less communicative days the General Register Office did not know as much about its customers as it now does). It is now possible for the General Register Office to supply statistical information on a wide range of topics and based on small areal units (as small as enumeration districts) in any desired format – print-out punched cards, computer tape – at a very modest cost to the customer. See Appendix B for a typical extraction. The customer can then use his own data-processing equipment to store this information and to compile statistical summaries for any desired combination of the chosen areal units, e.g. for special development. The General Register Office is able to undertake within a shorter time-span than would previously be contemplated the provision, at reasonable cost, of special tabulations for particular customers. As an example one may cite the provision to the Greater London Council of tapes with extra coding of workplaces to enable comprehensive workplace movement tabulations to be prepared based on the 1966 Census. These tabulations consisted of a set of matrices, one for each mode of travel, showing the number of journeys between each traffic zone of residence and each traffic zone of workplace; the traffic zone being a defined area comprising one or two districts. The tabulations were required to assess the traffic generated by the existing distribution of employment in Greater London, for development plan purposes.

In this way there has been a transition from the once-for-all analysis of the census records in terms of a rigidly pre-determined printed store, to the establishment of the census as a more dynamic data-bank that may be drawn upon continuously at comparatively short notice and in any desired format within the restraint only of the scope and continuity of the data-processing resources available to the General Register Office. Further reference will be made, later, to this consideration of continuity.

12. *New developments in census data-processing*

12.1 URBAN TYPOLOGY

There have been important developments in the exploitation of census material to produce an overall picture of a larger area in terms of the stereotypes into which smaller component areas can be fitted. While much has been done in the mapping of individual population characteristics to improve the visual representation of the variation, over a wider area, of an individual characteristic, e.g. proportion living above a specified housing density, conventional mapping breaks down when an attempt is made to deal simultaneously with several variables. Even if one takes as few as three variables (for example, the proportion of working age, the proportion leaving school later than age 15, the proportion in professional and managerial occupation) visual appreciation of any recognizable pattern of inter-area variation is difficult either by map or by tabular analysis. There are however more than a hundred variables normally available and of direct interest.

One is therefore faced with a mosaic of sets of variables to reduce to a summary. An obvious difficulty is the lack of independence of the variables. Any one variable could be used to group urban areas into classes or types but this same grouping would mask implicit similarities between urban areas in the same group in respect of other variables. If areas with high proportions of professional and managerial workers are selected they will tend also to be areas with low density housing, high educational standards, etc. If the association between two variables is strong then grouping by one is the same as grouping by the other. The problem is to find out how much really new information is obtained by introducing additional variables and in order to do this the degree of independence of the variables (or of groups of variables) has to be probed. It would be much more economical and achieve clearer discrimination to classify areas on four or five independent (i.e. orthogonal) axes than to unravel a skein of associations with a multiplicity of interrelated variables (non orthogonal).

An approach to this central problem can be made by the technique of principal component analysis. The aim of the technique is to concentrate the variables into a smaller number of transformed variables each of which is a linear combination (a weighted average) of some of the original variables grouped in such a way that each new variable is orthogonal. The technique thus aims to isolate *independent* components of the overall variability of the areas. If the analysis is successful, a few of the new variables (components) will account for the major part of the original variation among the areas examined. There is, however, the difficulty of interpreting the new variables. The original variables which are most strongly associated with the principal components can be examined to yield some interpretation of the content of the component. Thus, in a hypothetical case, a principal component analysis might explain the inter-area variation in forty or so census characteristics in terms, for example, of a population structure (age, sex, etc.) component, a household component, and a housing conditions component. There has been criticism of the method on the grounds that it is not robust; it may be sensitive to slight variations in input, even the inclusion or exclusion of one area.

An alternative technique which does not require a principal component analysis though it may be assisted by such an analysis, is referred to as 'cluster analysis'. This concentrates a larger amount of information about areas in terms of their scores on many variables to the single fact of the group to which they are allocated by the combined score. The method of grouping is determined by the object (use) of the analysis. Quite arbitrary procedures are often followed. Often it is not possible to arrive rigorously at a grouping which will fit a simple constraint, e.g. that intra-group variances are minimized. More often the definition of the groups can only be expressed in terms of the procedures used to derive them. The characteristics of the group are explicitly tabulated (as computer output) in terms of the scores of the contained areas on the original variables and this facilitates the interpretation of the 'type' represented by any group.

Use of these techniques has been given impetus by the availability of census information for individual enumeration districts to which reference has already been made. The population characteristics of a large conurbation area can be analysed in terms of the cluster grouping of thousands of enumeration districts instead of having to deal, as previously, with summaries, attributing false homogeneity, for the much larger component local authority areas. Important work of this kind has been going on in Birmingham, London, Manchester, Newcastle and other urban centres. Planning authorities find this kind of analysis useful for delineating areas within which there is real neighbourhood affinity and a common functional basis to the social entity thus defined. This helps to fix the location of administrative, shopping, and cultural centres. It can be a lead to the better management of local services and ultimately to local government re-organization. It also supplies a stratified sampling frame for many surveys and a better basis for differential population projections. It leads to the possibility that a large urban authority might eventually have available both a standard set of divisions of their area according to the more commonly used variables, and the ability to produce on demand divisions of the area according to variables which a particular administrative department or smaller authority might specify.

12.2 CO-ORDINATE OR GRID REFERENCING

As an alternative to tabular presentation census statistics can be represented pictorially by mapping enumeration districts and inserting census indices or colouring the districts to indicate the distribution interval within which the index for a particular district lies. The London Atlas is an important example (1968) of this technique. However the enumeration district has no natural shape. It represents a parcel of land chosen for the convenience of enumeration and it rarely conforms to a functional concept or to a socio-economic entity; moreover its size and shape changes from one census to another so that intercensal demographic changes are difficult to perceive. Since the basis of the enumeration district is census administration it is difficult to attain any functional or social conformity though an approach to this ideal has been made in the U.S.A. with its defined census tracts which are deliberately kept stable from one census to another.

An obvious alternative, to which the advent of the digital computer has lent impetus, is to assign parts of the enumeration district, even individual buildings, to the standard grid of the Ordnance Survey. One can go even further with the grid system and actually assign a co-ordinate fix to dwellings. Grid references or co-ordinates are digits. These digits can be stored with the associated census information. This makes possible the use of computer technology to produce an automatic computer output in map form. It is not however for automatic mapping alone that grid references are essential since it is possible to analyse any irregular area (e.g. an enumeration district) in terms of linear segments, the terminal co-ordinates of which can be handled by the computer and used to produce a map of the area; the process extends to effectively shading the area according to the associated demographic index. The main virtue of the grid is its immutability and its use therefore as a base for intercensal comparisons.

It is likely that grid referencing will become a standard census procedure, and it is almost certain that it will be used in the 1971 Census of Great Britain.

13. *Design of the schedule and testing procedures*

13.1 SCHEDULE DESIGN

In accordance with the author's philosophy that the design of any survey should begin with the output as related to *use* and work back to the questionnaire, this subject has been deliberately left to a very late stage in this manual.

We must emphasize once again that the census enumeration is an operation carried out simultaneously in all households as at a point of time and reliance is placed upon the accurate completion of a schedule of questions addressed to the head of the household. It is not a canvass-type survey with interviewers to assist in the interpretation of the questions and to write down the answers. There are 'enumerators', but they cannot do much more than deliver the correct type of schedule, collect it when complete and deal with the immediately obvious failure or inability to answer questions. While, at a later stage, there is some scrutiny of the schedules for completeness and the ultimate safeguard of computer editing, there can be little, if any, reference back to the respondent. Much therefore depends upon the drafting of the questions, and public understanding and acceptance of the concepts involved, and the overall question load.

We have already stressed that a most important issue is whether the official definitions and concepts are those which the public recognize in the normal course of their daily lives. Literally this means asking questions in common-sense terms (and it is a truism that surveys depend for their success upon common sense). But there is a little more to it than that. How is the official to be sure about the common sense of, for example, the term 'household'? In the last resort only the public can judge and their judgement will normally lead them to reject an official concept (e.g. the particular rules for making distinction between a boarder who is a member of a household and a lodger who is not) foreign to their own custom. This is likely to happen in spite of notes, instructions and Press and television publicity. Moreover, the error from this 'deviation' cannot be detected except in so far as the final census results may be clearly out of accord with the limited experience of other observations.

The actual drafting of the questions apart from the concepts involved is itself extremely important. Public co-operation cannot be expected to extend very far in the direction of reading long notes of explanation. The aim must be to frame a question in such a way that is both self-explanatory and concise. The hope is that a straight question will yield a straight answer. Ideally one would prefer questions that can clearly be answered by 'yes' or 'no', but that is impossible for almost all the topics comprised in the census enumeration.

Finally, another reminder that consideration must be given to whether the number of questions is within the limits beyond which irritation and weariness may react upon the quality of response and whether the physical layout of the questionnaire invites co-operative interest or engenders resistance, either by creating avoidable difficulty in comprehension or by sheer distaste.

13.2 PRE-TESTING

Since any other degree than the grossest failure to achieve these objectives cannot be detected in the final census results, when it is in any case too late, it is desirable to pre-test the questions and the enumeration procedure.

Ideally the pre-test would comprise an enumeration of a two-stage sample comprising a selection of a small number of households from each of a selected number of enumeration districts. The latter would be selected to provide a geographical spread and adequate urban/rural and socio-economic differential. At least two, preferably more than two, schedule layouts would be given equal representation, as would also different question designs. Completion by the householder would be followed by a re-enumeration by a trained interviewer. The difference between the incidence of a particular census characteristic as assessed at the first enumeration and at the re-enumeration (taken as the 'true' figure) would measure the 'error' introduced by the particular question design and layout combination after allowance for sampling errors. The scale of the operation is limited by the number of interviewers it is possible to deploy and, in practice, the sampling errors are uncomfortably, though not prohibitively, large.

Apart from the measurement of errors it is an integral part of this call-back technique that interviewers should discover the source of errors in terms of the ambiguity, obscurity or offensiveness of the original questions, so that the questions can be redesigned in order to obviate them.

In Great Britain until the 1966 Census, it was considered sufficient to rely upon the similarity in successive census schedules and the information carried forward from one census to another, and also upon small-scale tests carried out within the census staff and their families.

Prior to the 1966 Census, however, authority was given for a pre-test (Schneider, 1965) but the test was not held until 1964 when there was insufficient time to test the questions and schedule design. The pre-test was mainly concerned with the enumeration procedure and organization because the 1966 Census was the first to be held entirely on a sample basis, and it was important to guard against sampling bias. Even on this restricted basis it was deficient because the sampling frame was not tested in the field. The test was confined to procedures, instructions and forms by which the sample was to be transmitted to the enumerator, identified in the field and transformed into a set of records.

For the 1971 Census a number of pre-tests have been carried out and these have covered the content and drafting of questions, the design of the schedule, the enumeration procedure including the feasibility of grid referencing. No official reports of these pre-tests are, however, yet available.

13.3 POST-ENUMERATION SURVEY

Whether or not action taken as a result of these tests has been successful, and the final level of accuracy in response, can be assessed by an exactly similar call-back survey after the census enumeration.

For the first time in England and Wales such a post-enumeration survey was held following the 1961 Census. It consisted of two parts as follows: (1) A coverage check which would involve re-identification of buildings, dwellings and households in a random sample of some 2500 small areas distributed over the country. Each small area contained about twenty households. As a first stage sample 2500 ordinary enumeration districts were selected with probability proportional to expected size in terms of numbers of households. As a second each stage enumeration district was divided into ten parts by drawing a rough grid and one part was selected at random. This part was then adjusted to conform to observable boundaries. In these sample areas enumerators worked over the ground (effectively as at census day) very carefully and their estimates of the numbers of dwellings, households and persons were then compared with the original enumeration. (2) A quality check in which interviewers approached a sub sample of two households within each sample area and asked the census questions again with more careful preparation. Where there was a discrepancy between the original answer and the post-enumeration response an attempt was made to ascertain whether this was due to faulty question design, to inherent difficulty in the question, or real uncertainty about the situation in the household, etc. While organized as a separate operation this test was carried out by census officers and selected enumerators as soon as was practicable after census day (within days) and was, therefore, accepted by the public as an integral part of the census enumeration. It was conducted on a voluntary basis but under the same pledge of secrecy as the main census; response was almost complete. It was completed within three weeks of census day.

For a discussion of the choice of size of sample for the post-enumeration survey and the practical details of the sample construction and the survey procedure reference should be made to the General Report on the 1961 Census (General Register Office, 1968).

Several references have already been made to the results of the quality check part of this survey during the discussion of census topics. As to the completeness of coverage it was estimated from the survey that there was net under-enumeration of 0·2 per thousand population in England and Wales but the smallest of the sample was such that the true error had a 95 per cent confidence interval lying between net under-enumeration of 0·4 per thousand and net over-enumeration of 0·1 per thousand. These are *net* errors. In the sample 146,692 persons were enumerated and of these 209 were found to have been counted twice and a further 240 had been missed at the census. All these errors are relatively small. It would have been surprising had they been otherwise for a census held with a high degree of simultaneity in such a highly urbanized and densely populated country.

14. *Relationship of the census to vital registration*

The population changes from one census to the next as a result of the combined effects of births, deaths and migration. If the census interval is five years and if, for simplicity, the census date is assumed to be 30 June, then if

$$_y P_x = \text{enumerated population at age } x \text{ last birthday at the census in year } y$$

$$_y b_o = \text{births in year } y$$

$$_y d_x = \text{deaths at age } x \text{ last birthday in year } y$$

$$_y m_x = \text{net in-migration at age } x \text{ last birthday in year } y$$

then $_y P_x = {}_{y-5}P_{x-5} - \frac{1}{2}\left({}_{y-5}d_{x-5}\right) - \Sigma_1^4\left({}_{y-t}d_{x-t}\right) - \frac{1}{2}\left({}_y d_x\right)$
$$+ \frac{1}{2}\left({}_{y-5}m_{x-5}\right) - \Sigma_1^4\left({}_{y-t}m_{x-t}\right) - \frac{1}{2}\left({}_y m_x\right)$$

and where x is not equal to or greater than 5, the term

$\frac{1}{2}\left({}_{y-x}b_o\right) + \Sigma_1^{x-1}\left({}_{y-t}b_o\right) + \frac{1}{2}\left({}_y b_o\right)$ must be substituted for $_{y-5}P_{x-5}$. These relationships apply separately for each sex. They would require adjustment for a census date in April.

Thus $_yP_x$ may be checked against expectation as a test of consistency between the census enumeration and the records of births, deaths and migration and the previous census. In Great Britain where migration statistics are scanty, this test of consistency is, in practice, more of a test of net migration estimates than of the census enumeration. Such a check does however help to establish the extent of a common error in census enumeration, namely, the short fall of infants.

In 1921, 795,000 infants aged 0 and 826,000 infants aged 1 were enumerated, compared with 819,000 and 848,000 expected from registration records, a total error for the two ages of 46,000. It was thought that the error arose from difficulty in entering on the census schedule newly born children who were unchristened or unamed. In 1931 therefore a note was inserted to the effect that such infants should be described as 'baby'. As a result the error was reduced to 13,000 – 11,000 at age 0 and 2000 at age 1. In 1951 the corresponding deficiencies were 14,000 and 12,000, and in 1961, 11,000 and 12,000. The official figures for 1966 are not yet available.

When the age distribution of an enumerated population is examined a distinctive type of irregularity often becomes obvious; there are inordinately large numbers returned at ages with certain digital endings, especially 0 and 8, but sometimes at 5. It may be that where there is uncertainty as to age there is a tendency to approximate to the nearest ten or to an even number close to a multiple of ten. In addition there is an error arising from the fact that those within a short period of a birthday tend to return the higher age instead of the attained age. These errors have decreased at successive censuses in Great Britain. At earlier censuses there was some evidence (based on a comparison of the enumerated population with that derived from past births, allowing for mortality and migration) that females tended to understate their ages when approaching middle age. There has been much less evidence of this in recent censuses.

It must be borne in mind also that the census is related to vital registration data in another way. The census provides the benchmark for intercensal population estimates (Benjamin 1968) which in turn provide the denominators for births, deaths and other vital rates. Consistency is therefore essential.

15. *General organization*

In discussing the difficulties in 1961 and 1966 in Great Britain which were wrongly attributed to sampling rather than to inadequate groundwork, and, later, in discussing the need for more highly skilled local officers and enumerators, further reference was promised to matters of general organization.

It is a serious disadvantage that hitherto in Great Britain each population census has, traditionally, been treated as an isolated event. A further disadvantage arises from the loading of this highly technical operation upon the General Register Office which has always emphasized its allegedly administrative role and has never accorded first priority to the technological demands increasingly placed upon it. So far as the first defect is concerned, this means that the time-table suffers irreparably from the traumatic redeployment of staff that has to take place to provide the resources for this periodic 'extra'. Inevitably the process starts too late and takes too long so that there never is time to deal with all the contingencies that are likely to arise, or to plan really thoroughly. As to the second defect the major manpower contribution is drawn from the administrative staff of the General Register Office who do not have the professional training necessary to match the demands of skill stemming from a modern census with its wide scope and complex content, its utilization of sampling and its exploitation of the potential of electronic data-processing though fortunately some senior officers with invaluable experience survive from one census to another without falling victims to civil service mobility. These disadvantages have been mitigated to the extent that the shortening of the intercensal interval to five years has given a degree of permanence to the redeployment of staff. The need to prepare for 1971 before the 1966 Census could be disposed of was indeed foreseen by many as likely to force the issue of extemporization into the open.

It is significant that in 1961 and 1966, The General Register Office was so preoccupied with the time-tables for the basic operations that it made no attempt to fulfil its role as an interpreter of census statistics. The last commentaries on the census tabulations were those published in connection with the 1951 Census.

The same extemporization applies to that part of the census operation which once launched is largely out of central control (and therefore needs so much more careful planning), namely, the field work. As we have already stated, the registrars of births and deaths are not at present regarded as needing to be professional officers. Yet they are given, with little preparation, the task of supervising the field work and of recruiting and training the enumerators. In any case they cannot in present circumstances be redeployed from normal registration duties for sufficiently long to devote enough time and attention to the enumeration.

15.1 THE NEED FOR A PERMANENT CENSUS BUREAU

The logic of this situation is that there should be a permanent Census Bureau, embracing permanent local authority representation (either as part of or in parallel with vital registration staff) and supported by a permanent field survey force to which the census staff can have access at all reasonable times. This would provide continuing rather than extempore expertise. It would enable the work now peaked into short periods of pressure to be spread over the whole intercensal period and provide conditions for sound planning. It would provide opportunities for 'proving' contemplated methods. The field survey force would be essential to the provision of these opportunities as well as for monitoring the census and for post-enumeration tests. At other times it could be employed on current population survey work (labour force surveys, internal migration measurement, housing attitude surveys, household expenditure surveys).

15.2 OTHER POPULATION WORK

The population census does not stand on its own. Apart from providing up-to-date information on population structure, housing conditions, employment, etc., it serves as a bench-mark for intercensal population estimates and for population forecasts. In turn the population estimates serve as a control on the accuracy of the next census. For example, the estimates of error in the 1966 census depend largely on the estimated 1966 population brought forward from the 1965 estimate taking account of births, deaths and migration. In turn, the measurement of these elements of movement (births, deaths and migration) involves skilled analysis of the basic registration data and migration records and the appraisement of trends. If a permanent organization were to be created it would seem sensible to transfer the intercensal population analyses to it along with the population census.[1] This would bring together closely related procedures and would moreover effect an economical concentration of professional manpower.

---

[1] There might be a case for transferring such health statistics as still remain with the General Register Office to the Department of Health and Social Security and for absorbing in the same Depart-ment the remaining registration rump of the General Register Office since the present social security organization already embraces a form of registration system for insurance purposes.

15.3 OTHER CENSUSES

There are other censuses – of production, of distribution, of agriculture – and other census-type surveys, e.g. the condition of dwellings survey of the Ministry of Housing and Local Government, that involve similar expertise, viz. the correct identification of the unit (dwelling, household, establishment, shop) to be counted, agreement about concepts and definitions in which questions are to be phrased in order to produce the desired statistics, techniques of question design to ensure valid public response, large-scale data processing and skilled statistical interpretation. Moreover there is overlap of subject matter, e.g. employment and manpower, housing. These censuses are interlocked subject-wise and complement each other in many respects.

These censuses ought to be considered together in relation to their impact upon the public. They ought at least to be co-ordinated as to timing. Intercensally and at the time of the census they all need sample survey supplementation. They ought too to be brought together with the population census in the one permanent census bureau.

Although reference to practice elsewhere does not need to be used as an argument, the use of such permanent bureaux *is* the general rule in North America, in Europe and even in some less developed countries in Africa and Asia. Segmentation of censuses in Great Britain is an anachronism.

Appendix A: Sampling errors

The usual practice in sampling for the population census is effectively to list all households consecutively in the order in which they would normally be enumerated and to select every x^{th} household starting with the kth household where k is a random number $1 < k < x$ and x is the reciprocal of the sampling fraction.

Population

The variance to be attached to a sample estimate of population in Great Britain may be roughly calculated, if for example x is 10, as follows. Let n, h, p represent the sample numbers of persons, households, and persons per household and N, H the corresponding total numbers of persons and households

Then var n = var h.p.

$$= \left[\text{var h} + \left(\frac{H}{10} \right)^2 \right] \left[\text{var p} + \left(\frac{N}{H} \right)^2 \right] - \left(\frac{N}{10} \right)^2$$

On the basis of earlier census data, var p is of the order of 2×10^{-6} and N and H may be taken as 50 and 15 million, respectively. Var h can be shown, below, to be of the order of 12,000

$$\therefore \text{var n} = 4633 \times 10^3 \text{ approx.}$$

Thus the standard deviation of n is $2 \cdot 15 \times 10^3$, and since n is 5 million, this is $\cdot 043$ per cent approx.

Households

Let the number of households in an ordinary enumeration district be $[10t + y]$ where t and y are integers and $0 \leqslant y \leqslant 9$. Consider again a 10 per cent sample, for simplicity in demonstration of method.

Let k, where $1 \leqslant k \leqslant 10$, be the position of the first sample schedule. Then the deficiency w in the sample number of households will be

$$\frac{y}{10} \text{ for } 0 \leqslant y \leqslant (k - 1)$$

$$\text{and } \left(\frac{y}{10} - 1 \right) \text{ for } k \leqslant y \leqslant 9$$

The mean deficiency per district will be

$$\bar{w} = \begin{matrix} k = 10 \\ \Sigma \ N_k \\ k-1 \end{matrix} \left[\begin{matrix} y=k-1 \\ \Sigma \ {}_k n_y \\ y=0 \end{matrix} \left(\frac{y}{10}\right) + \begin{matrix} y=9 \\ \Sigma \ {}_k n_y \\ y=k \end{matrix} \left(\frac{y}{10}-1\right) \right]$$

where ${}_k n_y$ is the proportion of those districts to which k is applied, having a number of households with the last digit y, and N_k is the proportion of districts to which k is applied. The variance of

$$\bar{w} = \begin{matrix} k = 10 \\ \Sigma \ N_k \\ k-1 \end{matrix} \left[\begin{matrix} y=k-1 \\ \Sigma \ {}_k n_y \\ y=0 \end{matrix} \left(\frac{y}{10}\right)^2 + \begin{matrix} y=9 \\ \Sigma \ {}_k n_y \\ y=k \end{matrix} \left(\frac{y}{10}-1\right)^2 \right] \bar{w}^2$$

If the distribution of y and k are rectangular, then ${}_k n_y = 1/10$ and $N_k = 1/10$;

$$\text{then } \bar{w} = \begin{matrix} k=10 \\ \Sigma \\ k=1 \end{matrix} \frac{1}{2,000} [k(k-1)+(10-k)(k+9)-20(10-k] = 0$$

and var w =

$$\begin{matrix} 1 & k=10 \\ 10^4 & \Sigma \\ & k=1 \end{matrix} [285-10(10-k)(k+9)+1,000-100k] = \cdot 1650$$

In 75,000 enumeration districts therefore the deficiency in the number of households in the sample will have an expectation of zero and a variance of 75,000 ($\cdot$1650) = 12,375 or a standard deviation of about 110. This variance could be almost halved (i.e. var w reduced to $\cdot$085 if k were restricted to the complementary digits 5 and 6 ($\bar{w}$ still being zero), but this would be more difficult to organize in the field and a var w of $\cdot$1650 is small enough, since a deficiency or excess of 300 in a total of 1$\cdot$5 million is clearly tolerable.

Distribution of Population Characteristics

If, in an area j, the proportion of the population possessing characteristic i (where i may be age, occupation, etc.) is P_{ij} and n_j is the sample population for the region, f being the sampling fraction we may expect P_{ij} to be subject to a standard error of

$$\sqrt{\left[\frac{(1-f)\,P_{ij}\,(1-P_{ij})}{n_j}\right]}$$

if clustering effects can be ignored. For example, for a 10 per cent sample, if P_{ij} is ·05 and n_j is 2,500, this amounts to ·0041 or 8 per cent of the sample proportion.

Effect of clustering

The census sampling practice of selecting whole households rather than individual persons introduces an element of clustering which may tend to increase variances and to reduce the effective size of the sample. There is, for example, evidence (Hall and Glass, 1954; Benjamin, 1958) that, where the chief economic supporter of a household is a member of one of the professions, other members of the household are more likely than otherwise to enter the same or another profession, or, if not, to enter a managerial or administrative occupation. A household with one old person will be less likely than others to contain young persons, because two-generation or older generation families will predominate. Other restraints on the independent variation of members of a household doubtless operate. Many of them are avoided by using the whole household as a tabulation unit (e.g. housing, economic characteristics of households). For some characteristics, e.g. occupation, fertility, the cluster is smaller than the whole household. For the rest their effect is not likely to be of material consequence to the users of census tabulations. The investigations made in connexion with the 1 per cent household sample of the 1951 Census (General Register Office, 1958) indicated that for an individual characteristic such as age, the sampling errors were such as 'would have been applicable if the sample had been drawn at random with a person instead of a household as the sampling unit'. Compared with completely random selection, separate selection within each enumeration district involves geographical stratification which for some characteristics operates to reduce sampling variance, and to offset the effect of clustering.

Collective households

Where institutions are large enough to constitute a special enumeration district in themselves it is usual to select a person sample on the same consecutive basis as is used for households in ordinary enumeration districts. It is therefore similar to selecting households each invariably of one person. The above calculations of sampling errors should be correspondingly modified (for example, var $p = o$ and var $n = $ var h as applied to the number of special enumeration districts).

REFERENCES

BENJAMIN, B. (1958), 'Inter-generation changes in occupation', *Population Studies*, 11. pp. 262–68.

GENERAL REGISTER OFFICE (1958), *Census 1951 General Report,* London, H.M.S.O.

HALL, J. R. and GLASS, D. V. (1954), 'A Study of inter-generation changes in status' in *Social Mobility in Great Britain* ed. D. V. Glass, London, Routledge.

Appendix B: Census 1966

(see overleaf)

TOTAL PERSONS	PERSONS IN PRIVATE H'HOLDS	PERSONS IN Non-Pte. H'holds	No. OF PRIVATE HOUSEHOLDS	No. OF FAMILIES	No. OF DWELLINGS	ROOMS IN PRIVATE H'HOLDS	No. OF CARS

AGE	PRIVATE HOUSEHOLDS					NON-PRIVATE HOUSEHOLDS		TOTAL	1961 BASIS	1 PERSON	2 PERSONS
	MALES	FEMALES	MARRIED MALES	MARRIED FEMALES	OTHER MALES	OTHER FEMALES	MALES	FEMALES		1 ROOM		
0-4										2 ROOMS		
5-9										3 ROOMS		
10-14										4 ROOMS		
15-19										5 ROOMS		
20-24										6 ROOMS		
25-29										7 ROOMS		
30-34										8+ ROOMS		
35-39										TOTAL		

HOUSEHOLD FACILITIES — ROOMS (1961) — ROOMS (1966)

40-44										SHARING
45-49										NON-SHARING
50-54										TOTAL

HOUSEHOLD COMPOSITION — 2 PER H'HOLD

55-59									
60-64										HEAD OF HOUSEHOLD
65-69										CHILDREN
70-74										PARENTS
75+										OTHER RELATIVES
TOTAL										UNRELATED
15-59/64										TOTAL

CHILDREN	0	1	2	3	4	5	5-10	11-15	TOTAL
MALE									
FEMALE									
TOTAL									

DWELLINGS — TOTAL — HOUSEHN

SINGLE

BIRTHPLACE	MALE	FEMALE	TOTAL
COUNTY			
OTHER E.W.			
SCOTLAND			
IRELAND			
TOT. BR. IS.			
INDIA, PAK.			
BR. CARIB.			
AFRICA			
CYP., MALTA			
OTH. C'WLTH			
OTHER			

GARAGING	GARAGE IN CURTILAGE	GARAGED ELSEWHERE	PARKED IN CURTILAGE	PARKED IN ROAD	OTHER
1ST CAR					
2ND CAR					

CARS	ONE CAR	TWO CARS	OVER TWO CARS	TOTAL WITH CARS	NO CAR
HOUSEHOLDS					
PERSONS					

OCCUPANCY OVER 1.5 P.P.R.	2-PER H'HOLDS	3-PER H'HOLDS	4-PER H'HOLDS	5-PER H'HOLDS	6+ PER H'HOLDS
1961 BASIS					
1966 BASIS					

P.B. FLATS
WITH NON-RES.
CONV. FLATS
TOT. INC. CRVNS.

OCCUPATION — CLERICAL — TRANSPOR
MALE TOTAL
FEMALE MARRIED TOTAL / PART-TIME
OTHER FEMALE TOTAL / PART-TIME
ALL PERSONS

1-PERSON HOUSEHOLDS	15-59/64	60/65+	TOTAL
MALES			
FEMALES			
TOTAL			

HOURS WORKED	FULL-TIME	9-30	8 OR LESS	TOTAL
MALES				
MARRIED FEMALES				
OTHER FEMALES				
TOTAL FEMALES				
TOTAL				

EDUCATION — QUALIFIED — UNQUALIFIED
MALES
FEMALES MARRIED
FEMALES OTHER
TOTAL

2-PERSON HOUSEHOLDS	BOTH UNDER 60/65	ONE 60/65+	BOTH 60/65+
H'HOLDS			
MALES			
FEMALES			
TOTAL			

SHARERS	1/2 PERS H'HOLDS	3+PERS H'HOLDS
HOUSEHOLDS		
PERSONS		

ECONOMIC ACTIVITY	MALES	IN EMPLOYMENT			
		MARRIED FEMALES		OTHER FEMALES	
		PART-TIME	OTHER	PART-TIME	OTHER
15-24					
25-34					
35-44					
45-59/64					
60/65+					
TOTAL					

PERSONS PER ROOM	NON-SHARING		SHARING		TOTAL	
	H'HOLDS	PERSONS	H'HOLDS	PERSONS	H'HOLDS	PERSONS
1961 BASIS						
OVER 1.50						
1.01-1.50						
1.00						
0.75-0.99						
0.50-0.74						
UNDER 0.50						
1966 BASIS						
OVER 1.50						
1.01-1.50						
1.00						
0.75-0.99						
0.50-0.74						
UNDER 0.50						

S.I.C.	MANUFACTURE	CONSTRUCTION	UTILITIES TRANSPORT	DISTRIBUTION	FINANCE PROF. SERV
FULL-TIME MALE					
FULL-TIME FEMALE					
UNDER 30 HRS. MALE					
UNDER 30 HRS. FEMALE					
ALL EMPLOYED MALE					
ALL EMPLOYED FEMALE					
ALL TOTAL					

	4 PERSONS	5 PERSONS	6 + PERSONS	ALL H'HOLDS	1966 BASIS	1 PERSON	2 PERSONS	3 PERSONS	4 PERSONS	5 PERSONS	6 + PERSONS	ALL H'HOLDS
					1 ROOM							
					2 ROOMS							
					3 ROOMS							
					4 ROOMS							
					5 ROOMS							
					6 ROOMS							
					7 ROOMS							
					8 + ROOMS							
					TOTAL							

HENS (81)	KITCHENS (1966)	SHARED HOT WATER	NO HOT WATER	SHARED INSIDE W.C.	NO INSIDE W.C.	SHARED BATH	NO BATH/SHOWER	NO STOVE/SINK	NO FACILITIES	HOUSEHOLDS	PERSONS	FAMILIES

HOLDS	4 PER H'HOLDS	5 PER H'HOLDS	6 PER H'HOLDS	7 + PER H'HOLDS	16-24	25-34	35-44	45-59/64	60/65 +	MALES	FEMALES	TOTAL

SHARING HOUSEHOLDS	PERSONS	ROOMS (1961)	ROOMS (1966)	KITCHENS (1961)	KITCHENS (1966)	NO BATH/SHOWER	NO HOT WATER	OUTSIDE W.C. ONLY	ALL FACILITIES	NO FACILITIES	No. VACANT	ROOMS VACANT

MALES	SERVICE	ADMIN. & PROFESSIONAL	TENURE	HOUSEHOLDS	SHARING HOUSEHOLDS	WITHOUT INSIDE W.C.	WITHOUT HOT WATER	WITHOUT BATH/SHOWER	NO FACILITIES	PERSONS	ROOMS (1961)	ROOMS (1966)
			OWNED									
			RENTED COUNCIL									
			RENTED FURNISHED									
			RENTED UNFURNISHED									
			OTHER									

MIGRATION	UNDER 15	AGED 15-59/64 MARRIED MALE	FEMALE	OTHER MALE	FEMALE	60/65 + MALE	FEMALE	ALL PERSONS

HOUSEHOLD SPACES

ABSENT	
SHARERS	
NON-SHARERS	
OCCUPIED SPACES	
VACANT SPACES	
TOTAL SPACES	

OTHER

MALES	FEMALES MARRIED	OTHER

RESIDENT 1 YEAR AGO — SAME RESIDENCE / ELSEWHERE IN BOROUGH / IN COUNTY / IN S.E. / IN G.B. / OTHER

RESIDENT 5 YEARS AGO — SAME RESIDENCE / ELSEWHERE IN BOROUGH / IN COUNTY / IN S.E. / IN G.B. / OTHER

SOCIO-ECONOMIC GROUPS	ECONOMICALLY ACTIVE MALES	FEMALES	TOTAL	TRANSPORT TO WORK TRAIN/TUBE	BUS	CAR/M'CYCLE	FOOT	OTHER
PROF. WORKERS								
EMPLOYRS., MNGRS.								
OTHER SLF. EMPLYD.								
SKILLED WORKERS								
NON-MANL. WRKRS.								
SRVCE., S-SKLLD., AGR.								
ARMED FORCES								
UNSKILLED, ETC.								
ALL GROUPS								

MISCELLANEOUS SERVICES	PUBLIC ADMINISTRATION	OTHER

References

BENJAMIN, B. (1968), *Demographic Analysis,* London, Allen & Unwin.

GENERAL REGISTER OFFICE (1958), *Census 1951 England and Wales General Report,* H.M.S.O.

   (1959), *Census 1951 England and Wales Fertility Report,* H.M.S.O.

   (1966), *Census 1961 England and Wales Occupation Tables,* H.M.S.O.

GENERAL REGISTER OFFICE LONDON & EDINBURGH (1968), *Census 1961 Great Britain. General Report,* H.M.S.O.

HENRY, L. (1953), 'Fecondité des Mariages', Institut National d'Etudes Demographic, *Travaux No. 16,* Paris.

JONES, E. and SINCLAIR, D. J. (1968), *Atlas of London,* London, Pergamon Press.

MOSER, C. A. and SCOTT, W. (1961), *British Towns : a statistical Study of their social and economic differentials,* Edinburgh, Oliver & Boyd.

SCHNEIDER, J. R. L. (1965), 'The Census Pre-test of 1964', J. Roy, *Stat. Soc. A. (Gen) 128,* pp. 500–533.

UNITED NATIONS (1967a), 'Principles and recommendations for the 1970 population censuses', U.N. Statistical Office, *Statistical Papers Series M. 44,* U.N. New York.

   (1967b) 'Principles and recommendations for the 1970 housing censuses', U.N. Statistical Office, *Statistical Papers Series M. 45,* U.N. New York.

   (1968) Conference of European Statisticians. European Recommendations for the 1970 population and housing censuses. *Conf. Eur. Stats/W.G.6/115* and *Conf. Eur. Stats/W.G. 30/2.* Communicated to the author by the Economic Commission for Europe.